THE BIG THREE

THE UNITED STATES
BRITAIN · RUSSIA

BY

Yul'yevich

DAVID (J.) DALLIN

NEW HAVEN

YALE UNIVERSITY PRESS

1945

TO

M. M. B.

FOREWORD

THERE shall not, there must not, be a Third World War. The piled-up corpses of those who died in this war already reach the sky. Of ruins we have enough. Of misery we have more than one generation can endure.

To avoid armed conflicts, good will is not enough. Nor will it help if we shut our eyes, as many do, to the somber events which are transpiring in the international field, banish war from our thoughts, and reiterate words of peace. The road to war is paved with peaceful inscriptions.

The contrary is needed: a realistic appraisal of the new world which is now emerging, of the dynamic forces which are active in it, of the dangers which threaten at each turn. Sore spots must be studied, diseases must be called by their names. There is no greater crime against peace than willful shortsightedness in international affairs.

A correct evaluation of the new international situation is a precondition of sound policy. It is the only way of avoiding unexpected situations out of which we may awaken tomorrow to find ourselves in the midst of a new catastrophe.

Deep appreciation is expressed to Professor Harry Rudin of the Department of History, Yale University, for his cogent remarks and suggestions, and to

Mr. Eugene Davidson of the Yale University Press, for advice and for the interest that he has manifested in this book. The maps were prepared by Alexander Dallin and drawn by Henry Kelly.

D. J. D.

CONTENTS

MAPS

THE BIG THREE

I

THE CHANGING WORLD

"IT is a mistake to look too far ahead," Winston Churchill said upon his return from an important international conference early in 1945. "Only one link in the chain of destiny can be handled at will." At that time the war in Europe, this hardest part of the World War, was nearly won; the war in the Pacific was developing favorably. The next link in the chain of events would be forged tomorrow—yet legitimate questions had to be pushed aside. The conduct of the war was the paramount issue. It called for unity of purpose and the elimination of all other issues, doubts, and concerns as to the future of the world, the future of Europe, and particularly the future of the British Empire. Out of this necessity for singleness of purpose emerged the coalition of the Big Three.

This stage of history has ended, at least in Europe, and a new link in the great chain is taking shape. Now, to "look ahead" is no longer a mistake, it is a duty and a need. The great question is whether the Big Three alliance, born in 1941, will continue. What conditions are necessary for its continuance? And what if it does not last? It is not only natural but essential to look ahead and to attempt to discern the pattern of the next link, to ask questions, and to act in accordance with the answers. The questions concern both the character of the Big Three's wartime solidarity and the divergence among many of their interests; the might of their combined forces, and the relation of their separate powers; the bright prospects of victory and the hardships and crises which will follow.

Great Powers have been born in wars; they have matured in wars; and they have died in wars. War lays naked to the world the developments and evolution within individual nations which were too gradual to have been observed in normal times; international crises reveal their strengths and weaknesses. Within the past few centuries once great powers—Portugal, Sweden, Holland, Spain, Turkey—became minor nations following a war. The minor powers of yesterday—the United States, Japan—have grown to be great. The forging of history continues and the next link of the chain will soon be fashioned. Who will be the masters of tomorrow? Will the powers defeated in this war be eliminated forever? Will the victors retain their combined dominance over the world?

In ancient days one great power existed at a time. With the rise of the nation-states during the last few centuries the normal order has been the coëxistence of a multitude of great powers. The idea of the great powers of ancient times was domination of the world—of their small world, which seemed so enormous to them. In our times the scheme is division of the world.

Neither the scheme of dominance of past epochs nor the present scheme of global division has been able to prevent incessant internal and external crises in the course of which old powers declined and new ones came to the fore.

In modern times, until the beginning of the twentieth century, only the nations of Europe were able to attain to the stature of great powers. During the eighteenth and nineteenth centuries there were five of these: Great Britain, France, Austria-Hungary, Russia, and Prussia-Germany. For a certain time Italy was able to play a great-power role; Spain, too, descending slowly from her state of greatness, was still active on the periphery of the family of great powers. Essentially, however, five nations shaped the world. They fought each other to achieve higher rank among the great or to avoid relegation to lower rank. In general, it was not the defeat itself, the heavy human losses, and the devastation, which led to relegation to the role of a small power. After France's unprecedented losses and crushing defeat during more than two decades of revolutionary and Napoleonic Wars, she rose again in a surprisingly short time. Central Europe, devastated in the Seven Years' War, was soon again the realm of two mighty nations, Prussia and Austria. It was only when there was internal weakness within a nation, or when decisive changes occurred in the general international situation, such as the shift in world trade routes from the Mediterranean to the Atlantic, or when new inventions made production of

3

coal and iron a prime element of military power, that former great nations declined and new ones inherited their thrones. It was under such conditions that England rose to be a mighty empire and Germany grew to be the strongest power on the continent.

The great revolution in power relationships occurred around 1900. Europe's total dominance was at an end. An American and an Asiatic nation were rapidly acquiring wealth, military strength, and influence in international affairs. The growth of these two nations brought unfamiliar problems and created new foci of tension. The Far East, secondary or even third rate in world affairs a few decades before, was becoming a new battlefield both in war and in peace. Its emergence created an upheaval in the international position of a number of nations, Russia among them. It would be too much to say that the center of gravity had shifted away from Europe. Rather there was now more than one center of gravity and the importance of the new ones in the twentieth century grew with every decade.

Austria-Hungary was struck off the list of powers in 1918, Italy in 1943. In 1940 France was dealt a blow which rendered her impotent for a time. Germany and Japan have already been or are in the process of being relegated to inferior status. Only three nations have survived the lethal epidemics of the twentieth century: the United States, the youngest among the powers; the British Empire, former Ruler of the Waves; and Russia, an old and at the same time a young nation. These three were the only nations interested in both the old European theater of affairs and the new one in the Far East.

Along with the Big Three, the new organization of the United Nations is often referred to as a new great power in the world. This conception is erroneous. The United Nations, a great world organization, will be, it appears today, but a treaty of the Big Three, with all the virtues and weaknesses of international treaties. According to the narrow form which it is taking, it will actually be an agreement of the three powers to attempt a peaceful settlement of disputes, whenever possible. To this limited extent it represents a forward step, as do the other agreements on international collaboration—the Air Convention, Bretton Woods, Chapultepec.

The frequently drawn analogy between the organization of the United Nations and the United States is not a correct one. The United States emerged as a superstate uniting individual states into one power, the individual states conceding to the superstate the privilege of maintaining an army and navy and of conducting their foreign affairs. Nothing of that nature is proposed for the United Nations; there is no great nation in the world which is prepared to concede to the organization of the United Nations the operation of its navy, its air force or army. A world superstate is not on the agenda. Even the Soviet Union, with her program of ultimate inclusion in the Union of the

5

other nations of the globe, is not prepared to create such a superstate by agreements with other powers.

The United Nations will be able to prevent military action between small powers, in cases of conflicts among small nations which do not have the backing of one of the big. In all other cases, namely, those in which a great power is interested in the affairs of a small nation, or in which disagreement among the great powers has reached a stage where no compromise is possible, the United Nations will be as helpless to prevent wars as was the League of Nations. The United Nations will have neither a policy of its own nor a separate military force to achieve its lofty goals.

There is even danger inherent in the exaggerated hopes which have been pinned on the new international organization. Decisions arrived at by the Big Three, decisions which may have imposed injustices and sacrifices during our time, are sometimes accepted by public opinion with the implicit or even the expressed hope that the organization of the United Nations will be able fundamentally to alter them in the future. People are inclined to expect that the new United Nations will open an era that will achieve abolition of "power politics," revision of unequal treaties, liberation of oppressed nations. Nothing of the kind is likely to occur. What has been lost today will not be recovered by the new organization tomorrow; injustices will not be redressed by speeches at the sessions of the new organization. "Power politics" will operate within the new United Nations organization as it has outside it. The influence of the organization on the course of history will not be distinct from or additional to the influence of the heterogeneous powers which will guide its course.

In the present global conflicts a multitude of wars were merged into one great war; the outcome of that war must answer a multitude of questions. China's war against Japan and against foreign privileges; Britain's war against the hegemony of any other nation in Europe and the Far East; Poland's centuries-long war for independence against Germany and Russia; the American war against domination in the Pacific and the Far East of any other power and for a stable Europe; Russia's war of self-defense; the Soviet war for a world-wide Union; the French war against the "hereditary enemy"; the wars of Balkan States for territories and predominance; Rumania's war for Transylvania; Australia's war for security and Oceania; Germany's war for half the world; Japan's war for the other half—these and a hundred other problems tied up in this bloodiest of all conflicts of history will have to be solved today and tomorrow. Many of them concern the relationship of the allies to the enemy. Others concern relationships between the allies themselves. The first ones must be solved by the sword. The latter ought to be solved by peaceful means. Whether or not they will be solved by peaceful means, and under what conditions a peaceful solution of them is possible, is the greatest problem for the immediate future.

The course of history speeds onward, great events follow on each other's heels, and already new life springs from the ruins. Today nothing is more important than to discern and to study the first contours of the next link in the chain of our common journey.

II

THE UNITED STATES AND BRITAIN

IT was not until half a century ago that the United States rose to the rank of a great power. Continuing her growth during the period between the Spanish-American War and the end of the second World War, she has become, within a period of about fifty years, the strongest among the strong, the greatest among the great powers of the world.

Rivalry among the powers for top places existed in peacetime as well as in war, not only between the adversaries in the conflict but among the allies themselves. Before Pearl Harbor Britain occupied first place. In the short space of three war years America outflanked her in the big race, and since 1944 has assumed the leading place. She will hold this place not during the period of the war only but in the postwar period.

America outstripped Britain, first, in the most decisive field of naval construction and operation; second, in size and equipment of land armies; third, in tonnage of commercial vessels; and fourth, in the amount of supplies shipped to allies all over the world —she has not only "financed the allies" but furnished Britain the chief means for continuing the fight. In addition, the relatively insignificant lowering of the American standard of living during the war is proof that, if necessary, her war strength could be increased.

The most striking index of the growing power of the United States is the development of her naval power. In 1942–43 the Navy of the United States, for the first time in history, surpassed the British Navy, both in tonnage and number of naval vessels. Since 1943 it has continued to expand at a faster rate than the British Navy, and by 1945 the difference in strength between the two achieved striking proportions.

In January, 1939, the tonnage of the British Navy, the largest in the world, was 1,351,430 tons. At that time the United States possessed approximately 330 fighting ships, with a tonnage of 1,213,790.

After five years of war the British Navy has restored its heavy losses and even to a certain extent augmented its prewar strength. The American Navy, however, was growing at a quite different speed. American naval construction amounted to 785,208 tons in 1941; 1,597,754 in 1942; 3,556,903 in 1943, and 5,457,490 in 1944. Plans for 1945 called for construction of 4,096,000 tons.[1] Combat ships built in 1941–44 had a tonnage of 3,571,010 tons. In 1945 an additional 1,116,000 tons had to be constructed.

On January 1, 1945, the United States Navy had 11,707,000 tons afloat; 61,045 vessels, including 1,167 warships. Compared with 1939, the navy has increased more than fivefold. During the war America

1. Official data. *New York Times*, December 30, 1944, and February 1, 1945.

also developed her particular brand of combined sea-land warfare: amphibious operations on a large scale and the use of a special fleet for amphibious warfare; prefabricated ports transferred by sea to a foreign land and glued to the shore; and last, but not least, extensive use of aircraft.

Naval aircraft has likewise surpassed the naval aircraft of any other nation. Production of aircraft (for the navy alone) amounted to 3,638 planes in 1941, 30,070 in 1944. The program for 1945 called for 28,-591 naval planes. If it is true that "this war is a war of motors," as Stalin said in one of his wartime speeches, then Detroit has become the capital of the world.

In the 1940's the only important navies other than the American were the Japanese and the British. The size of the American Navy as compared to these two has been stated by Secretary of the Navy Forrestal: "This nation, at the end of 1944, will have naval power and accompanying air power to match the naval forces of the rest of the world." "New ships are wanted," he said, on January 31, 1945, "to maintain the margin of superiority we now have." [2]

Construction of new combat ships will not cease in 1946 and 1947. If Japan loses her navy at the end of the war, or before, America and Great Britain will possess war fleets in a relation to each other of two to one, or perhaps even of three to one. Such a development will be tantamount to a revolution in international relations.

2. *New York Times*, April 3, 1944, and February 1, 1945.

THE UNITED STATES NAVY

THE various international agreements for collective limitation of naval force concluded between 1922 and 1939 have left a bitter taste, and there is prevalent in the United States a firm determination to maintain naval supremacy after the war. In 1944 Secretary Forrestal outlined the government's program in these words: "Whatever international agreements or associations may be sponsored by the United Nations, one of the cornerstones of peace must be the maintenance of armed forces by the United States, more particularly, maintenance of the sea power."

In the course of the two decades between the World Wars, he says, "we scrapped and sunk thirty battleships, fifteen cruisers, 139 destroyers, 52 submarines. This shall not happen again." [3] Public opinion must be influenced to prevent the new naval power from being dissipated because "peace not backed by power remains a dream, in Churchill's phrase." [4]

An indication of public opinion on the subject of maintenance of naval power was afforded in the replies made by thirty-seven United States Senators, of both political parties, to questions put to them by the Navy League in May, 1944. They revealed a strong feeling that the United States fleet should be maintained after the war as the largest and most powerful in the world. There was unanimous agreement that the

3. *Saturday Evening Post*, February 24, 1944.
4. *New York Times*, April 4, 1944.

country must "be judge of its needs" and wary of naval limitation treaties. Senator Byrd advocated "the largest and most powerful navy in the world" and "the greatest air force in the world." Senator Vandenberg wrote: "There must never again be a moment when we are not equal to the total defense against any potential enemy."

Neither the Senators nor the Secretary of the Navy mentioned Britain, but certainly they had Britain in mind when they said that the United States must possess "the greatest navy in the world" (Senator Tom Connally, Chairman of the Foreign Relations Committee) and must "remain what it is today—the most powerful and efficient naval force in the world" (Senator Davis).

"I certainly do not want," wrote the then Senator Truman, "to sink the Navy as we did before when we got inveigled into a disarmament conference."

"We must not repeat the expensive and vicious limitation of arms treaty of 1922," replied Senator Kenneth McKellar, Chairman of the Appropriations Committee.

"The Presidents of the future," Senator Walsh said, "must risk unpopularity and criticism, they will be called warmongers and alarmists," but they will have to sustain a powerful navy.[5]

There cannot be any doubt that the United States will maintain naval supremacy after the war. When

5. The replies of the United States Senators are quoted from the *New York Herald Tribune*, May 28 and June 4, 1944.

dangerous enemies are out of the way, expansion may cease and a certain amount of reduction may be effected, despite the Senators' wartime declarations; but there will be no retreat from the position of supremacy. The postwar world will have to accept the fact that naval supremacy, for the first time in centuries, is not in the hands of Great Britain, and has passed from Europe to America. This development, a logical consequence of America's economic and political growth, is bound decisively to alter relations between the English-speaking nations.

In the field of the merchant marine the tonnage of the United States grew rapidly during the first World War, from 5,600,000 tons in 1914 to 15,000,000 in 1920 (including the Great Lakes fleet); it had dropped to 12,200,000 tons by 1939. But during the present war years it has expanded enormously. In the three years from January 1, 1942, to January 1, 1945, 43,-671,794 deadweight tons in 4,319 vessels were added to the merchant fleet of the United States. Allowing for substantial war losses, the fleet will embrace, after the war, "fifteen to twenty million tons operating, with another twenty million tons in untouched reserve to cut into former Axis markets." [6] About half of the fleet consists of vessels which will not be suitable for postwar trade. Recently, however, designs of cargo ships have been altered to make them suitable for postwar operations. The huge 20,000,000 ton

6. Vice-Admiral Emory Land, War Shipping Administrator, quoted in the *New York Times*, January 4, 1945.

"merchant reserve" would be a "sanctuary," according to the official statement of Admiral Land.

The development of Britain's merchant marine has been of a different character. In 1939 the British merchant marine was still the largest fleet in the world, with a total tonnage of 17,500,000 tons. Of this amount, 11,600,000 tons—about two thirds—were lost before January 1, 1944. Shipbuilding was accelerated, and between 1939 and 1944 Britain produced 4,700,000 tons. Some of the newly built ships, however, are unsuited for postwar trade. Available shipping at Britain's disposal, including the fleets of smaller allies, amounted to only 13,500,000 tons in 1944.[7]

The United States Office of War Mobilization has published the following estimates of postwar tonnage of merchant shipping: the British Empire, 20,000,000 (compared with 24,000,000 in 1939); the United States, 60,000,000 (12,000,000 in 1939).[8]

The emergence of the United States as first among the great powers is bound to lead to significant and often unexpected consequences.

It is only natural that New York should take the place of London as the financial capital of the world and that the headquarters of the future monetary world organization should be located in America. No peace settlement after the war will be possible without America, nor any maintenance of these settlements

7. *Facts about Britain's War Effort*, pp. 11–12. British Information Service, November, 1944.

8. *New York Times*, February 18, 1945.

without her continuing participation. America in the
future will have to take part in every important international affair, at times perhaps even against her will.
This is one of the burdens that must be borne by a
great power. In a quarrelsome family of nations a nation cannot at one and the same time be both the
strongest and the most passive member of the family.
Whether Democrats or Republicans rule in the White
House, whether an imperialist or a moderately pacifist
tendency prevails, a policy of intervention in one
form or another will be the rule, and aloofness from
world affairs the exception. The time will have passed
when a choice between intervention and isolation will
be possible. Persistent effort and even wars are the
price that nations pay to secure their status as great
powers, and once they achieve such a status, wars become a must, and the road back to safe old isolationism
is barred.

It is therefore shortsighted to expect that America
is headed for a long period of peace after this war. The
opposite would appear to be the truth: there will be
deliberate or undesired conflicts; prompt or reluctant
intervention in international political affairs; small
military expeditions; merely naval operations; or great
bloody conflicts calling out sea and land forces.

During the nineteenth century the United States
waged three international wars of moderate proportions, in all of which the human casualties were probably less than those during one week of the invasion of

Europe in 1944.[9] During the same century Great Britain waged twenty-seven wars. Only forty-six entire years of that century were years of peace for Britain. At times two and three wars were being waged simultaneously. They ranged from the gigantic anti-Napoleonic campaigns to the smallest of expeditions in Burma and Africa. Every world event was Britain's concern. Britain was not ruled during that century of almost uninterrupted wars by bloodthirsty, war-loving autocrats. The leaders of the nation were often classic liberals, with faith in conciliation through free trade and an abhorrence of war. Democracy in England developed, and the arts and sciences flourished. The national wealth mounted and the British standard of living was envied throughout Europe. In view of these conditions British wars cannot be considered as silly adventures of unreasonable minds. Some of them were necessary for the survival of Britain in her role of leading power; others were waged for reasons of expansion and conquest.

To a certain extent the situation of Britain during the nineteenth century is analogous to that of any nation which occupies a leading position in world affairs, and will likewise apply to the nation which supplants England as the strongest naval power. Of course this is true only to a degree. It is true that the British Empire is dispersed over five continents and possesses an

9. In the Mexican War, 5,823 killed and wounded; in the Spanish War, 289.

unprecedented multitude of interests, but this fact does not represent a basic difference between England and other leading nations and does not affect the fundamental character of a great sea and world power as far as its obligations and interests are concerned.

SEA POWER

HALF a century has passed since Vice-Admiral Alfred T. Mahan published *The Influence of Sea Power upon History*, and the passionate discussions that the book aroused have gradually subsided. There has survived however from the tempestuous arguments over Mahan's writings a realization of the peculiar and decisive role of sea power in history.

Continental nations, particularly those on the European continent, have been inclined to identify military power with land power: infantry, cavalry, artillery, and aviation. Only a small part of their youth serve in their navies; only a minor part of their military expenses are allotted to the naval forces. Their wars have been chiefly land wars, and their great battles mostly land battles. That the role of leading nation should go to a purely sea power was almost incomprehensible to them.

The fundamental difference between land and sea power is demonstrated in the fact that even backward nations have been able to achieve predominance as land forces but never as sea powers. Huge armies of Mongols, Tatars, Turks, advancing from the East to the West, were able to annihilate European states of advanced civilization and to create new empires of their own. Such primitive but powerful advances from the East again frightened Europe a few decades ago and the "yellow danger" was often the subject of political discussions. Even today a similar fear is based on the notion that mere numbers, millions and millions of armed men, may prove more powerful than the trained, well-equipped but relatively small armies of the Western Peoples.

Naval power, however, has never been created or developed by backward nations; in invasions carried out by backward nations the sea coast, once reached, was the limit. Naval power is a product of advanced technics; its creation and especially its rapid expansion during wartime are possible only for the most advanced of nations. Ghengis Khan, Tamerlane, Attila were able to build continental empires, and the Turks knocked at the gates of Vienna a few centuries ago; but none of these masters of war was able to produce sea power of any importance.

The leading nations of world history have without exception been the possessors of great naval force, and the strongest of the sea powers has always occupied first place among the great powers. Not every great power is a great naval power. Austria-Hungary, for instance, even at the peak of her strength, did not possess a large navy. Nor did Russia possess a great naval force. Except for a period of two decades (1900–1918) Prussia-Germany, although one of the greatest of European powers, was not a great naval power. But

The Big Three

Spain, Portugal, France, the Netherlands, Britain, succeeding one another as top naval power, all occupied places in the front row of the nations of the world.

It was of course the sea power of Britain that administered the coup de grâce to the formidable forces of Napoleon. The combined navies of four nations defeated Russia in 1855 and the defeat gave a strong impetus to the abolition of serfdom and to other internal reforms. Exactly half a century later Japan's sea victories provoked the first of the eruptions that culminated in the Russian Revolution. America's sea power, having defeated Spain, opened the road to American activity in the Far East. Britain's sea power made certain Germany's defeat in the first World War. The sea power of Britain and America have doomed Germany in the second World War, and even Russian successes in this war were made possible only because her allies dominated the seas so that uninterrupted streams of supplies from America and England reached her.

It has always been true that the leading naval power has been the richest and the most highly industrialized nation of the world. Capacity for naval building goes hand in hand with resources in money and goods, and this combination likewise entails a powerful potentiality for coalition building. Loans and subsidies made by sea powers helped to equip and to arm continental armies. Britain, the great sea power, was also the world's banker. British gold and notes cemented British coalitions at times when, to use the famous French phrase, three things were needed for a war: money, money, and money. The word "soldier," from the Latin *soldum* (pay), means "hired man," and often the size of a hired army, a privilege of rich governments, corresponded to the amount of available gold.

Because the strongest navy always belonged to the nation that was farthest advanced technically and economically, there has been only infrequent shifting of maritime power. It would be difficult to say whose land armies during the last century were the most powerful, Russia's, Germany's, or France's. First place was occupied at times by one and at times by another of these nations. Once defeated in war and relegated to a back place among the powers, each soon acquired new force, which was followed by a new shift in their power relationships. No development of this kind has been possible among the sea powers. A nation that once attained dominance of the seas entrenched itself on the oceans with a tenacity unknown and indeed impossible to be achieved on dry land.

For two centuries Britannia ruled the waves. Except for her defeat by America in the Revolutionary War, Britain had not known a defeat in any war for a quarter of a millennium. After all, the oceans comprise two thirds of the surface of the globe, and he who dominates this vast blue expanse in addition to possessing land force has attained a position of exclusive superiority in the world.

NEPTUNE'S FAREWELL TO BRITAIN

In *The World Crisis* Winston Churchill recalls his first visit to Portland, where the British Navy lay. His yacht was surrounded by the great ships, "so vast in themselves, yet so small, so easily lost on the surface of the waters. On them floated the might, majesty, dominion and power of the British Empire . . ." And then he says: "Open the sea-cocks and let them sink beneath the surface, and in a few minutes, half an hour at the most, the whole outlook of the world would be changed. The British Empire would dissolve like a dream . . . the central power of union broken."[10]

But a great navy is not enough, Churchill said. "A command of the seas and oceans" means possession of the greatest navy in the world as a precondition of the existence of the empire. The navy produced by Britain became the builder of the empire. Now the empire lives or falls with the navy.

The traditional "two-power standard" of the British Navy meant that it must be at least as large as the next two largest navies combined. Every school and university student in England has been taught that a navy of such size is a necessity for the nation. Britain's reserves of food have never exceeded a seven weeks' supply, and her reserves of some important raw materials can be exhausted very rapidly. A blockade of

10. Winston Churchill, *The World Crisis,* I, 123.

England, if successful, would mean defeat, starvation, disintegration of the empire. Unlike other nations, the empire can live only under conditions of British naval supremacy throughout the world. These facts have been burned into the minds of all Britons. In all negotiations involving navies they have preached this doctrine.

It was inevitable, therefore, that he who possessed the next strongest navy to Britain's should be Britain's Enemy Number One and must reckon with an eventual war with Britain. The sole exception was the United States. This exception was not dictated by sentimental reasons. It was true that the sea power of the United States grew stronger between 1900 and 1914, but, coincidentally, Germany was beginning to rise, and Germany was near by and dangerous, whereas America was remote. Besides, the American formula of a "navy second to none" in the first decade of this century remained merely a slogan, while Germany was actively challenging Britain.

In 1914 the United States, as a navy-building nation, was potentially stronger than Germany and potentially as strong as Britain herself. Actually, however, the American Navy at that time amounted to 1 million tons, as compared with the 2.7 million tons of Britain and the 1 million tons of Germany.

During the World War of 1914–18 Britain was indisputably first in actual sea power. In 1916 the United States decided to start construction of a great new navy which, had it been completed, would in a few years have upset all traditional British-American naval relationships. The program was not carried out, however. When the United States entered the war it was in the common interest that she postpone the building of large combat ships and concentrate instead on small units and on ships for the merchant marine. The result was that at the end of the war, when the German Navy had ceased to exist, Britain possessed forty-three large warships (dreadnoughts and cruisers) and the United States seventeen; Britain 425 destroyers, America 172. Japan had meantime been accelerating her naval construction and advancing to the front row of naval powers.

In 1918, on the eve of the armistice, there occurred a heated discussion between London and Washington concerning freedom of the seas, mentioned in Point Two of President Wilson's Fourteen Points. The British Government sensed in the statement a challenge to its supremacy on the seas. Wilson's adviser, Colonel House, insisted that "the United States and other countries would not willingly submit to Great Britain's complete domination of the seas any more than to Germany's domination of the land . . . If challenged the United States would build a navy and maintain an army greater than theirs."

A few days later Lloyd George countered, saying: "Great Britain *would spend her last guinea to keep a navy superior to that of the United States* or any other Power, and no Cabinet official could continue in the

Government in England who took a different position." [11]

A few days later the armistice was signed. Britain's situation became more difficult when the United States resolved, after the armistice, to take up again the naval program it had planned. The specter of approaching naval inferiority again frightened Britain. In 1919–20 naval tonnage under construction in America was three times the amount under construction in Britain and twice that of Japan. If development at this pace continued for only a short period, the United States would become the greatest naval power in the world.

The nervousness within Britain was far greater than was generally known at the time. Colonel House again discussed the question with Lord Robert Cecil at the time of the Peace Conference, and what Lord Cecil said and wrote to his American interlocutor acquires great interest in the light of events twenty-six years later.

"In Britain," Lord Cecil wrote in April, 1919, the impression prevails that "the American ambition is to have a navy at least as strong or stronger than that of the British Empire." He proceeded to describe "the British sentiment about sea power":

It has been for centuries an article of faith with every British statesman that the safety of the country depends upon her ability to maintain her sea defence, and, like all deep-rooted popular sentiments, it is founded on truth.

11. Charles Seymour, *House Papers*, IV, 160, 179.

Not only have we dominions scattered over the face of the world . . . but the teeming population of the islands of the United Kingdom can only be fed and clothed provided the avenues of sea traffic are safe. We import four-fifths of our cereals, two-thirds of our meat, the whole of our cotton and almost the whole of our wool. If we were blockaded for a month or less, we should have to surrender at discretion. That is not true of any other country in the world to the same extent.

Least of all is it true of the United States, which could, as far as necessities of life are concerned, laugh at any blockade . . .

If I were British Minister of the Navy and I saw that *British naval safety was being threatened, even by America,* I should have to recommend to my fellow-countrymen to spend their last shilling in bringing our fleet up to the point which I was advised was necessary for their safety.

Cecil's arguments, which were those of the British Government, were not accepted by President Wilson, and only a vague promise of periodic consultation was given. Lloyd George was anxious, relates Charles Seymour, to receive a positive endorsement of Great Britain's special maritime position, and perhaps a guarantee that the United States would not push naval competition to a point where she would threaten *the supremacy of the British on the seas.* "The American delegates refused to promise that the American fleet should always be inferior to the British." [12]

12. *Ibid.,* IV, 417–423. (The italics are mine, D.J.D.)

These conversations were the genesis of future conferences on limitation of navies. The first of them was the Washington Conference in 1921–22. At that time Britain already had to accept the fact that a sea power had arisen which could not be reduced by either peaceful or warlike measures. Instead of the traditional "two-power standard," the British Navy had to be content with the "one-power standard," meaning equality with another naval power.

Equality of the British and American Navies had to be conceded in 1922. Japan's ceiling was fixed at 60 per cent of the British (or American) Navy, and France's and Italy's at 35 per cent. Following the unsuccessful conference of 1927, the London Conference of 1930 established a better relation of ship types for America. When Japan quit the naval conferences in 1936 and declined even to give information about her naval construction, the era of limitation of navies was over.

The American Navy had not reached its status of equality without strong opposition from Britain. This opposition never developed into a bellicose attitude toward America. Forced to maneuver between Germany, Japan, and the United States, Britain had to acquiesce in the extensive American naval construction. It was the only reasonable policy. Germany and Japan could be defeated just as France, Russia, and Turkey had previously suffered defeats at the hands of Britain. But a defeat of America in the twentieth century was out of the question.

Then came the second World War, when the British Isles, in a struggle against an upsurging Germany and Japan, were only too happy to find in America a powerful ally capable of naval expansion. Old standards, agreements, slogans, and postwar considerations had to be pushed aside. The war had to be won. The logical consequence was a second decisive shift in sea power as between the two nations in the years from 1941 to 1945. This shift, representing an American victory of the first magnitude, has been accomplished in an atmosphere of alliance, with the consent of the defeated and with his thanks, mingled, probably, with some bitterness.

FALSE PROGNOSES

FOR two decades political observers and scientific researchers have been predicting that an Anglo-American war in the near future was unavoidable. Were not North American and British industries engaged in a life and death struggle in the South American markets? Was not the naval competition an irreconcilable situation? Has not the American principle of freedom of the seas often cut across British blockades and barriers in times of war? Scholarly studies and statistical tables were used to demonstrate the inevitability of an Anglo-American war.

"War between America and Britain," wrote the intelligent author of a voluminous investigation of British-American relations, in 1930, "is more probable

than war between America and any other power." [13]
The well-known former French delegate to the
League of Nations, Henri de Jouvenel, predicted that
in the next war, which he foresaw would occur in
1935, "the United States would not be on the same
side as Great Britain." [14]

In Moscow there was even more emphasis on this
inevitable war, which fitted into the picture of deep
antagonisms in the capitalist world, and particularly
into the Russian concept according to which Britain,
"the greatest suppressor of backward peoples and their
revolutions," had to be badly beaten by a capitalist
rival. Trotsky was the first to proclaim (in the '20's)
that a future Anglo-American war was a certainty.
He rightfully boasted, in the '30's, that Stalin and the
party had adopted and developed his idea. Acceptance
of this "scientific foresight" was imposed upon every
Communist when the Sixth Congress of the Communist International unanimously resolved that "Anglo-
American collaboration has turned into a furious
Anglo-American rivalry which opens the prospects of
a huge conflict" and that "the Anglo-American antagonism is the main antagonism in the imperialist
camp." The chief exponent of this concept was Stalin.
"The principal conflict between capitalist rivals," he
said, "is that of the United States and Britain . . .

13. Ludwell Denny, *America Conquers Britain* (New York),
p. 3.
14. *New York Herald Tribune*, November 26, 1927.

What is this basic conflict fraught with? It is fraught with war. When two giants collide with each other, when this globe is too small for them, they try to measure their strength, they try to solve the vexing question of world hegemony by means of war." [15] The Moscow economic expert, Professor Eugen Varga, wrote in 1933 that "the inevitability of a war between Britain and the United States is clear to us; [16] the war between Britain and the United States is certainly bound to develop into a world war." He went on scientifically to preview the composition of the future anti-American coalition: "the four-power pact of Britain, France, Germany and Italy." On the other hand, "an Anglo-American coalition against Japan is practically impossible . . ." Palmiro Togliatti, the Italian Communist leader, told the Congress of the International in 1935 that "the antagonism between Britain and the United States is the most profound of all the antagonisms tearing the capitalist world apart."[17]

History took another course, thus once more making a laughingstock of "scientific" soothsayers.

15. Stalin, *Problems of Leninism* (1931), pp. 335 and 494.
16. L. Ivanov, *Anglo-American Naval Rivalry* (Moscow), Foreword.
17. *Pravda*, August 18, 1935.

III

AN ANGLO-SAXON SUPERSTATE?

THE internal evolution of the British Empire and the relationship between the United States and Britain have given rise to new trends and tendencies which are bound to play a decisive role in the emerging political structure of the world. The time has long passed since British Crown colonies were attached to the mother country by "ties of blood" or by sentiment. One after another these colonies have developed into separate nations with their own trade systems, peculiar political problems, and international interests.

Since the '50's and the '60's when Canada acquired self-government and independence in her trade policy, there have been predictions of an imminent breakup of the empire, or at least a secession of its English-speaking colonies. The old phrase ascribed to Turgot has been repeated again and again: "Colonies are like fruits which only cling till they ripen." Since the second half of the nineteenth century, British Governments, in order to preserve as much as possible of the unity and strength of the empire, have been cautious in opposing tendencies toward autonomy in the colonies. In 1887 colonial conferences were instituted in England; they prove to have been the first steps on the long road to the status of equality for British colonies.

In 1907, at the fifth Colonial Conference—now referred to as Imperial Conference—the British Government proposed the constitution of a permanent Imperial Council. The plan was rejected chiefly because of the opposition of Canada. But from that time on the term "dominion" was substituted for the somewhat humiliating "colony." In 1911 for the first time the governments of the colonies were let into the secrets of Britain's foreign policy. In the war years 1917–18 their delegates constituted the Imperial War Cabinet.

Then came Canada's revolutionary act in 1918: she demanded participation as an independent state at the Peace Conference. As a result of this demand the dominions were represented at the peace table and were signatories to the Versailles Peace Treaty. The treaty granted certain of them "mandates" over former German colonies. Thus the dominions became complicated state structures. Within the League of Nations the dominions participated as individual nations. Since 1923 they have been negotiating and signing treaties with other nations directly, without benefit of the medium of the Foreign Office in London. It was only logical that they should begin to dispatch their own envoys to a growing number of foreign capitals.

The famous Imperial Conference of 1926 stated that "every self-governing member of the empire is now the master of its destiny," and proclaimed the do-

minions "autonomous communities within the British
Empire, equal in status, in no way subordinate to one
another in their domestic or external affairs, though
united by a common allegiance to the Crown, and
freely associated as members of the British Commonwealth of Nations." Finally, the Statute of West-
minster of 1931 was the last step on the road from
inferiority to equality. A treaty or alliance entered
into by the London government was no longer binding upon the dominions; the engagement by Britain
in a war no longer automatically involved the dominions. No taxes paid in the dominions were reaching
the British Treasury. Now it was the British Crown
that legally united these independent nations in one
Empire. At times it seemed that the centrifugal forces
had outstripped the centripetal ones. Why should
New Zealand need a common political roof with Newfoundland? Why should the monarch of London be
acknowledged as the head of the state in Pretoria?
Were not the troubles of the Canadians different from
those of the Australians?

The British Empire, so strange, so unique a phenomenon in world history, nevertheless continued to
exist. How united an empire it really was would become evident when it became involved in a great war.

The London government did not consult the dominions in 1914 when it declared war on Germany;
the dominions could not be forced to join. They
joined the next day, however. And again in 1939,
when they had full independence, they joined in

Chamberlain's war declaration. While in near-by France some people protested "Why die for Danzig?" on the other side of the world Australians and Canadians, with little understanding of the situation in the Polish Corridor, were sending their sons to the North African desert to fight Germans and Italians. Only one of the dominions, Eire, asserted its independence and remained neutral in 1939, thus placing the King in the paradoxical position of being a belligerent in London and a neutral in Dublin. Eire, however, was the only exception.

THE BRITISH EMPIRE

Two forces were holding the independent dominions together and binding them to Great Britain: first, the military defense offered by the British Navy; and second, the opportunities for expansion and prosperity within the empire. An additional motive was the granting, during certain periods, of preferential tariffs to the dominions.

The British Empire has represented a useful and beneficial alliance. Individually the dominions, with their limited means, could not create the military force which might one day be needed if any of their territories were menaced. And who could give better protection than the greatest sea power in the world? Australia in fear of the yellow race; South Africa standing amongst the controversies of the British, Dutch, and Germans, and with the former German colony under her control; Canada, relatively secure but situated between two oceans of potential danger—all of them stood ready to contribute in blood if necessary in order to enjoy a guarantee against the possible threats facing them. Indeed, who knows what would have happened to these small nations if they had been exposed to invasion by Britain's rivals, France, Germany, or Japan, in the nineteenth and twentieth centuries?

"If we had declared for neutrality," the Premier of the Union of South Africa told his Parliament on November 3, 1939, "we would have no protection on the seas, no transport, no communications and no market." Were it not for British naval protection, a German coup would certainly have taken place either before or during the war in the territories of the former German colonies in Africa.

Defense of her colonies by Britain was axiomatic during the nineteenth century. Their land forces were too small to be of use in large-scale war, and their navies could never attain the size of the fleets belonging to the great powers. "Local defense," of course, was organized by the dominions, even a "local navy" for patrol duty. But their defense was dependent and has remained dependent on the protection of a big navy. In time of war all their small navies had to unite under British command. This system of defense as far as the British colonies are concerned was the best one so long as the British Navy was the world's greatest.

However, the question of defense did not become

important, so far as the future dominions were concerned, until the last decade of the nineteenth century. No serious military threat faced them. It was, on the contrary, the empire that sometimes needed colonial troops for its colonial wars (for instance in the Sudan, in the '80's).

In general, until fifty years ago, the future dominions were small in population and did not play a very significant role in the international policy of the mother country. In the '90's the population of Australia amounted to 3 millions, that of Canada 5 millions; and the total population of all the future dominions was 11 to 12 millions. Most of their growth in population and influence occurred in the twentieth century. The population of all the dominions is now about 35 millions, and the dominions today are the most active and valuable part of the empire. In size of population they are rapidly approaching Great Britain (47 millions). The importance of the dominions has grown much faster than their population.

During the last few decades some of them have begun to form British Empires in miniature. Australia and New Zealand, with their mandated colonies, have developed into a politically vital center of Oceania; their sphere may considerably widen after the end of the Pacific war. The Union of South Africa is going through a similar evolution; the many British possessions in Africa, south of the Equator, are in a way its "sphere of influence." Only Canada has had no important opportunities for expansion.

An Anglo-Saxon Superstate?

The bearer of new ideas for the transformation of the British Empire was General Smuts, and at present it seems that his visions may become reality in the approaching postwar period, after there has been a reshuffling of relations of the great naval powers. Smuts called for the reconstruction of the empire (as well as of the colonial policy of other nations) on a regional basis: the small colonies of each region to be grouped around the larger dominion and entrusted to a regional council.

"Isolated colonies belonging to a mother country," the Premier of South Africa wrote in 1942, "should be grouped into larger units both for more efficient and economical administration, and for larger-scale development of policies common to all." He suggested the creation of a council in each region in which "not only the British government as the parent state but also the unit itself and any interested neighboring British Commonwealth, such as Canada, Australia, New Zealand and South Africa" would take part. The United States too, he said, should be a member of the council.[1] The dominions would develop, in such a case, into three world centers of English power, wealth, and civilization. With the exception of India and the Middle East, most of the rest of the Empire would fall into one of the three spheres.

"To the Union of South Africa," General Smuts said in April, 1940, actually opening a new campaign in favor of his Pan-Africa, "all Africa south of the

1. *Life*, December 28, 1942.

37

Equator at least, and especially the British territories, are a matter of economic interest and concern . . . I come to stress once more . . . the Pan-African idea, if I may call it so . . . More and more the countries north of us are looking to us for guidance in various directions . . . our neighbours, South-West Africa, the Rhodesias, Portuguese East Africa, Kenya, Tanganyika, Uganda, and the Belgian Congo." [2] General Smuts in these plans goes, of course, beyond the limits of the old empire and prepares to annex non-British lands.

Australia and New Zealand were the first among the dominions to understand the change that had taken place in the relationship of the powers. In this war the British Navy has not been able to defend them against the great conqueror of the Pacific. Had it not been for American aid, Australia, New Zealand, and Oceania would have been conquered and subjugated by a ruthless enemy. Occupied in the Atlantic, Britain would not be in a position to give adequate protection to South Africa, either.

John Curtin, Prime Minister of Australia, said in a speech on December 14, 1943:

"Australia and New Zealand are autonomous nations in proximity to the colonies of powers whose seats of government are located in other continents. They are in a preëminent position to speak with au-

2. J. C. Smuts, *Toward a Better World* (New York), pp. 215, 217, 221.

thority on the problem of the Pacific and have a primary interest in their solution . . .

"If Britain, Australia, Canada and New Zealand are to develop an understanding about a common policy on their mutual interests in the Pacific, it is equally logical that they should collaborate in a regional organization with other nations who have parallel interests in this region."

The new trend of thought in the dominions is toward a combined protection of the dominions by America and Britain and a new form of relationship between the solid old empire and the young American Republic.

"The dominions endorse (at present) even more heartily than before participation by the United States in regional and general security plans." [3] The fear of remaining in an "exclusive British bloc," so new and so characteristic in our time, is almost universal in the dominions of the far-flung empire. "Australians look for a consultative council of all Pacific powers and to an effective American leadership." [4]

The trend toward a British-American-dominions combination is strong in South Africa, too. "It appears to me," General Smuts wrote, "that the United States of America should in the future have a direct say with the mother countries in the settlement of general colonial policies . . . I have no doubt that a

3. *Foreign Policy Report*, December 1, 1943.
4. It was only because of Australian and New Zealand demands that the American, General MacArthur, obtained supreme command in the British lands and waters of the South Pacific.

partnership of the United States in overhead colonial controls would be cordially welcomed as far as the British Commonwealth of Nations is concerned." He foresees even "a corresponding decrease of power exercised in London." [5]

Canada tried, long before the other dominions began to advocate activity by the United States, to play the role of a mediator between London and Washington. A sort of military alliance was concluded in August, 1938, between Canada and the United States, when President Roosevelt declared that "the United States will not stand idly by if domination of Canadian soil is threatened by any other Empire," and the Canadian Prime Minister replied that "enemy forces should not be able to pursue their way either by land, sea and air to the United States across Canadian territory." [6] However, without America, but backed by American guarantees, this ally of the United States went to war a year later as a member of the British Commonwealth.

In 1940 a Permanent Joint Board of Defense was created by Canada and the United States, and Prime Minister King emphasized that this agency was not for wartime purposes only. "It is the enduring foundation of a new world order." A plan of common defense was endorsed in the spring of 1941: the United States was to protect and defend Greenland, whereas the defense of Iceland and Newfoundland was to be organized jointly by Canada and the United States.

5. *Life*, December 28, 1942.
6. *International Conciliation*, March, 1944.

Air bases for the United States were to be set up on Canadian territory.[7]

This penetration by the United States deep into the British Empire was of course in accordance with the wishes of the dominions and with the consent of the London government.

In view of the state of affairs that has been described, what is the future of the British Empire? If the American Navy has become a magnet attracting small powers, what will become of the proud Commonwealth?

THE FUTURE OF THE EMPIRE

THREE different answers to these questions are possible, and all of them have been proffered by British leaders on different occasions.

One concept views the development as a mere wartime exigency; when the war is over the dominions will have to revert to their former condition and unite again with the British motherland. This point of view, expounded by Lord Halifax in 1944, met with immediate repudiation. Lord Halifax pointed out that in a new world, after this war, Great Britain alone, without the dominions, will be small and weak compared to the other great powers; its future would be uncertain, its possibilities limited. Britain will have to fulfill a difficult task in Europe, and "Western Europe will look to her for leadership and guidance." But to accomplish this task Britain needs the constant assist-

7. *Ibid.*

ance of her dominions. Lord Halifax's idea therefore was: "Not Great Britain alone, but the British Commonwealth and Empire." [8] A few days after this speech Prime Minister King rejected Lord Halifax's concept. Instead he advocated "close collaboration not only inside the British Commonwealth but also with all friendly nations, small as well as great."

A second suggestion was that of a close union of Great Britain with some small West European nations, especially Belgium and Holland. However, this British "sphere of influence" on the continent of Europe, if it materializes at all, will necessarily be limited to a few small nations; neither France nor even defeated Italy can be possible components. It is clear that such a combination would in itself be no match for the other great powers and would not solve the difficult problems of Britain.

The third suggestion, a plan which has never been presented as a complete scheme, is the most important. It recommends some form of lasting military collaboration between America and Britain. Like every plan in British history, the proposal starts off tentatively, with practical questions. Only in the implications it raises is its significance apparent.

After his first Quebec Conference (1943) with President Roosevelt, Prime Minister Churchill suggested the extension of military collaboration between the United States and Britain to the postwar period.

"In my opinion," he said, in his address at Harvard

8. Speech in Toronto, January 24, 1944.

University, "it would be a most foolish and improvident act on the part of our two governments, or either of them, to break up this smooth-running and immensely powerful machinery [combined Chiefs of Staff] the moment the war is over . . . We are bound to keep it working and in running order . . . probably for a good many years."

Combined military machinery in peacetime may be called an international police force, or the military force of a combined superstate, but it must imply concord between both governments in their foreign policies. There is more in this project than a proposal of a mere alliance of two national governments.

"The great Bismarck—" Churchill added, "for there were once great men in Germany—is said to have observed toward the close of his life that the most potent factor in human society at the end of the 19th century was the fact that the British and the American peoples speak the same language. That was a pregnant thing." In the postwar world "nothing will work soundly or for long without the united effort of the British and American people. If we are together nothing is impossible. If we are divided all will fail."

Some of the technical details of the Anglo-American superstate machinery had been elaborated by the then United States Secretary of the Navy, Frank Knox, who, with President Roosevelt's consent, discussed them in London, where they met with approval. His idea was that the military collaboration of the two nations in the postwar period start with naval collaboration—the American and British Navies to patrol all waters, the American forces chiefly the Pacific and a part of the Atlantic (the more northern waters around Greenland and Iceland as well as the more southern waters); Americans and British to share bases where units of both navies are in operation. (These joint bases used during peacetime would mean a further step on the road to collaboration).[9]

It is strange that these significant proposals have been only rarely and briefly mentioned in the world press. Public discussion of them has not even begun. The real cause of the unusual silence has to do mainly with the wartime alliance of America and Great Britain with Russia. A tightening of American-British ties could create the impression that the two powers are entering into a solid coalition against the only other great power—Soviet Russia; that the first contours of future conflicts are being drawn in these blueprints; and it might offend and alienate Russia if her allies started preparations leading toward a separation from her. As an intelligent observer of Anglo-American relations remarked in May, 1944: "The nations of the British Commonwealth may seek a wider basis for security in some form of an Anglo-American coöperation. But this threatens to divide the world into two rival camps, the Anglo-American versus Russia." [10]

9. *New York Times*, May 3, 1944.
10. Frank Underhill, in *The Nation*, May 6, 1944.

An Anglo-Saxon Superstate?

THE THREE SORE SPOTS

IT is literally true that Britain lives on the supplies she receives via the sea routes, and that if she were effectively blockaded she could not survive. For centuries no sort of blockade of Britain has succeeded; neither Napoleon's continental system, nor Wilhelm II's "reckless U-boat war," nor Hitler's submarines were able to achieve the goal of cutting Britain off from the world. The Royal Navy, stronger than all its opponents, has smashed all attempts to blockade Britain.

Everything changes when a new sea power, stronger, perhaps twice or three times as strong as Britain, begins to sail the high seas. In a war with the United States Britain would be doomed and a defeated Britain would become the easy prey of a blockading power. For this reason the Government of Britain after this war will, and for an indefinite period must, avoid serious conflict with the United States. Britain will give way rather than take her chances in a fight with the United States.

This state of things imposes limits on British peace-time foreign policy. Britain must avoid diplomatic or military action which is contrary to the interests or world policies of the United States. Real freedom of action is possible for Britain only in spheres in which America is not interested; in other words, considering the far-ranging interests of the United States, in spheres of only minor importance. On vital questions

45

London will have to coördinate its political course with, and in certain cases even subordinate it to, that followed by Washington. The situation implies, on the other hand, that America will in a sense incorporate in her own policies the demands of British interest, not only those of the dominions but those of Great Britain. Such a combination of interests, in which the American ones would be superior, would have a different effect in different spheres of British international activity.

Three main spheres of British grand policy are of chief importance for American and for the postwar world in general: the Far East, the Middle East, and Europe. In these three regions British-American collaboration, if it arises, will meet its first tests.

1. In the Pacific and the Far East, American predominance will be most pronounced. In accordance with the respective roles played by Britain and America during wartime, Britain will have to make corresponding sacrifices of many a tradition and will have to subordinate her activities to the policies of the United States.

Differences between British and American policy in the Far East have been obvious for half a century. While Britain has waged several wars against China, the United States has remained aloof from military operations.[11] Britain has shared territorial spoils with other powers, but the United States has had no part

11. It did take part, however, in the collective action of the powers during the Boxer rebellion.

in these divisions. As far as Japan is concerned, America never went as far as Britain in collaborating with the "Britain of the East." Britain had a solid alliance with Japan, but not so America.

The relatively small narrow strip of land and ocean from the Philippines to Vladivostok is the only corner of the world where the Big Three, plus Japan, France, and China, possess territories which make them near neighbors. From the French colonies in the south to Japan in the north, this part of the globe is acquiring a growing importance. In no other part of the world have the changed relationships among the powers been so obvious as in the Pacific and the Far East. British military force can never again attain the importance it possessed in the East only a short time ago. American policy will play the dominant role.

2. In the Middle East collaboration with Britain would pose two problems for America which formerly preoccupied Britain.

For almost a century Iran and Afghanistan have constituted 'buffer states" at the approaches to India. In the last few decades Iran and Iraq have acquired a growing importance because of their riches in oil. In the '30's the whole of the Arabian peninsula, too, became an important source of oil output. This situation has brought about the conversion of this part of the world into a domain of classical "oil diplomacy," international intrigue, and struggle. In this part of the world purely economic foreign concessions developed into problems of international policy.

American capital has recently become interested in the oil industry of the Middle East and this interest is bound to develop further. Such a development would bring America nearer to the hot spot of Anglo-Russian controversy, antagonism, and intrigue. If Anglo-American collaboration should become an organic thing, American international activity will more and more have to share with Britain the burden of Central Asiatic conflicts.

The second great problem confronting Britain in Asia is India. India is, of course, an internal problem of the British Empire, but India is also a great world problem. Sentiment in America has always been strongly pro-Indian, and the pitiable situation of India's people has aroused anti-British feeling in this country. A general British-American peacetime collaboration would make changes in India inevitable.

3. The third great field of British activity—and of a possible sphere of Anglo-American collaboration—is Europe. The situation in Europe is, in one sense, the opposite of that in the Far East. In Europe Britain has, during the course of centuries, elaborated her policy relating to every European problem down to the smallest and least important detail.

What has been and what is British continental policy?

IV

FACING THE CONTINENT OF EUROPE

PRINCIPLES and ideology have been alien to British international policy. Britain would have perished long ago if she had undertaken to conduct her foreign affairs and to select her allies in accordance with any ideology, political scheme, or religion. In her relentless struggle for existence and power she has had to accept every ally and to buy assistance with her gold whenever this could be done.

Britain has never waged a war for democracy. Nor has she waged wars in the name of aristocracy or of autocracy. She has at times been an ally of autocrats against democracies; in other cases she has assisted democracies against absolutist rulers. Britain has never waged a war for Christianity against paganism or Mohammedanism; nor has she waged wars for Protestantism against Catholicism or Orthodoxy. She was first an enemy and then an ally of Catholic countries, of Orthodox peoples, of Mohammedans, and of pagans. Nor has Britain conducted wars for capitalism against feudalism or Communism or any other social system. She has managed throughout the course of her history to be the ally of any system when necessary, and to fight the same system by every means when her situation so required. "England has no permanent friends, she has only permanent interests," Lord Palmerston once said.

Britain hated and ridiculed the French kings, but when the French achieved liberty, equality, and fraternity, she sharpened her weapons and plunged into a series of new wars against the Revolution, since it still was France. She heralded the liberation of Orthodox Greece from the Ottoman yoke, but soon afterward waged a war in common with the Sublime Port against the Orthodox Empire of the White Tsars. She was an ally of Tsarist Russia in 1914–16, but greeted the Republic warmly in 1917; then in 1918 in Siberia she again aligned herself with the Tsar's generals against the remnants of democracy.

The legend that Britain, in her almost constant antagonism to Soviet Russia over a period of two decades, was guided by ideology—for capitalism against Communism—is misleading and harmful. It was not Communism or Sovietism or the advocacy of abolition of private ownership that alienated British policy. The principles of Communism would not of themselves be sufficient to provoke London's hostility any more than were dozens of other principles of other foreign nations in the course of the centuries. Actually it was the extension of the new Russian policy into Europe and Asia which aroused Britain. To this the Labor governments of Britain were opposed to no less a degree than those of the Conservative party.

No principles in foreign policy—this has been the only British principle. International relations in peacetime as well as in war have been an incessant, day-and-night struggle; lack of allies might mean defeat; inertia might mean death. Scrupulousness in selection of friends and fastidiousness in selection of means might lead to a catastrophe. High principles have been out of place in British policy.

One maxim of British policy, however, was crystallized out of experience centuries ago: the strongest state of Europe is the chief enemy of Britain. It must be fought without respite. Periods of peace are periods of preparation for wars against Britain. The enemies of the strongest state are Britain's friends; the successes of the strongest state are Britain's sorrow; its misfortunes Britain's fortune.

This maxim is today more valid than ever.

BRITAIN AGAINST THE STRONGEST POWER

IT TOOK Britain two centuries to rise to the height of the power she had attained at the beginning of the twentieth century. The first half of this two-hundred-year period was occupied with a fight against the then most powerful force of the world—France.

Today the history of those times appears the history of a British obsession. Generations of Britons were born, grew up, and died with the notion that France was the greatest evil in the world. Behind each political move in any corner of the world London suspected a French plot, or intrigue, or anti-British coalition. Wherever Britain made a step she encountered French trade, French pioneers, French colonies,

French occupation, or French allies. In India the French were entrenched before the British and it took a series of bloody wars to expel France and to secure India for Britain. In North America France was powerful, too. Louisiana was a French stronghold. In Europe French splendor and power attracted allies and frightened enemies. The great wars which Britain waged in the eighteenth century were wars with France, no matter what their official label. In the War of the Spanish Succession it was France, not Spain, that was Britain's target. In the war of the Austrian Succession London fought not so much for Austria as against France. In the hard and sanguinary Seven Years' War nothing was of such importance to England as the fight against France, the head of the enemy coalition. In the American Revolution Britain and France took opposite sides, and Britain's new war against France, in 1793, was the revenge for French assistance to the American colonies in their fight for independence. Britain fought France during the latter's revolution and during the Napoleonic Wars almost uninterruptedly for twenty-two years. France had no more troublesome enemy than Britain at that time: uncompromising, ruthless, treaty breaking, creating one coalition after the other, financing every foe of France in every corner of the world.

Britain was the greatest sea power, France the greatest land power, and their struggle should have provided an answer to the paramount question of modern times—which is stronger, land or sea military power?

Facing the Continent of Europe

In 1814–15 France was decisively defeated by British coalitions. For Britain this was the end of a conflict that had lasted since 1689. Never since has France been able to rise to her old stature and to threaten British interests to the extent that she had. From now on there occurred periods of improved and periods of worsened relations with France, even of warlike moves but on the whole France had receded from the first place that she had occupied in British international relations.

A new mortal enemy was rising in the meantime, a new power which was about to assume the same place in the nineteenth century that France had occupied in the eighteenth. This was Russia. Only a short time before, Russia had still been a nation of the European Far East, somewhere on the periphery of modern history. Then she moved quickly to the west and acquired enormous territories; in a series of wars she manifested great military potentialities. At the same time she started to move into Central Asia, endangering the approaches to India. Within a few decades Britain was meeting Russia in all parts of the world of those days. In 1750 the Russian frontier lay 1,200 miles from Europe's center at Berlin. In 1790 the distance was only 1,050 miles; in 1800, 750 miles; in 1815, 200 miles.

The Black Sea was essentially a Turkish sea before 1780. Turkey, having frittered away her aggressive force during the preceding century, presented no great danger to Britain, which preferred that Turkey rather than a European power be in possession of the approaches to India. But in 1792 Russia won a large piece of territory on the Black Sea. She moved simultaneously against Persia—also lying on the road to India—and annexed her northern provinces. Finally, Tsar Paul, in a fit of political madness, launched a military expedition against India. It collapsed before the Russian Army reached the Indian border, but the new role of Russia was now manifest. Every step taken by Russia was a step against Britain. The British Ambassador was involved in the assassination of Tsar Paul.

Siding first with Britain's enemy and then with Britain, Russia, at the head of a coalition, subsequently administered the decisive blow to Napoleon in the war on land, and Tsar Alexander drove into Paris, the greatest of victors in the eyes of the liberated peoples. Russia had become the first continental power in Europe, and annexed Finland, Bessarabia, and the greater part of Poland. The Tsar founded and led the Holy Alliance, while Britain and France remained outside it.

Russia became strong in the south and southeast, too, in the direction of Turkey, Persia, and Afghanistan. The Near East and Middle Asia were at that time already spheres of British influence and every Russian success was a British defeat. The Caucasus was conquered and Russia took in more territory around the Black Sea, menacing British predominance in the Eastern Mediterranean. In the 1840's Russia conquered Turkestan. In a new war with Persia she acquired exclusive rights in the Caspian.

Facing the Continent of Europe

During the Revolution of 1848–49 the Austrian Emperor asked for Russian help against the uprising in Hungary, and an army of 100,000 men under General Paskevich appeared at the gates of Budapest. The revolutionary movement in Rumania was also crushed with Russian help. Central Europe was feeling the superior force of the Russians. The fear of Russia on the part of the conservative governments mingled with the hatred of liberal and revolutionary elements; Russian policy in the former Polish provinces, after the Polish uprising of 1830-31, added fuel to these sentiments, and Polish émigrés in all parts of the world represented a living argument against Russia's internal and external political course.

Then followed the consequences that are inevitable when one growing and expanding military power begins to menace her neighbors as well as her great rivals. A coalition of Mediterranean forces, the creation of which would have been impossible a few decades earlier, was formed. Britain sided with France; Turkey, Britain's enemy in the recent conflict revolving around Greece, found her way into this anti-Russian coalition. With the added participation of Sardinia, the coalition defeated Russia in the Crimean War in 1856.

Russia's advance to the south was checked for a time, although her army retained its full strength. Britain's antagonism toward Russia, which continued her rapid expansion in Central Asia, did not diminish. In the early '70's Russia agreed not to take Khiva and Afghanistan into her sphere; but in 1873 Khiva was occupied by the Russian Army and practically annexed to the empire. In 1856 Russia signed a treaty forbidding her to have a navy in the Black Sea. In 1870 she confronted England with a *fait accompli* and became a naval power in the south.

In the Russo-Turkish War of 1877–78, which ended in Turkey's defeat, Britain's sympathies lay on the Turkish side. Now Britain executed by purely diplomatic means her master stroke. This was the brilliant Victorian Age, when Britain was at the peak of her power and Disraeli was leading his empire from one success to another. Russia was compelled to offer to the Berlin Congress for discussion her peace treaty with Turkey. England, France, and Austria-Hungary compelled the Russian Government to agree to a revision of the treaty which reduced Russian gains substantially. Furthermore, Britain succeeded in virtually obtaining from Turkey the island of Cyprus, thus rounding out her possessions and her bases in this part of the world where the Russian offensive was strongly menacing British interests.

In the meantime the Suez Canal had been built, and this spot, where Europe, Asia, and Africa meet, was acquiring for Britain a growing importance. This was another reason for her growing antagonism to Russia. During the '80's Russia moved deeper into the Trans-Caspian regions and when she occupied Merv, bordering Afghanistan, Britain was reported becoming very "mervous."

In the '90's Russia (an ally of France in 1894)

erected the Trans-Siberian railroad. Here again Russian expansion encountered British interests and Britain's opposition. Russia was emerging as one of the most active of the Far Eastern powers. When Manchuria and Korea were for all practical purposes brought into the Russian sphere of influence and further Russian penetration into China appeared probable, Britain concluded with Japan an alliance aimed against Russia. Japan's war against Russia in 1904–5 was Britain's war, and the victories were British victories. Again Britain had succeeded in defeating Russia by means of the military force of her allies.

The defeat in the East and the growing revolution inside Russia were in Britain's eyes symptoms of a weakening of Russia's aggressive power. In a measure the "Russian problem," as viewed by the British Empire, appeared to have been solved. For the moment, Russia no longer represented the greatest danger.

From the British point of view this defeat of Russia occurred at just the right time, because another nation was rapidly rising to the rank of a first-class power and now endangered British interests more than did defeated Russia. The rising nation was Germany.

The acute stage of Russo-British antagonism, having lasted for about seventy-five years, was superseded by a German-British rivalry which had been sprouting in the meantime. It was Germany now that occupied first place in Britain's policy. It was of particular importance to Britain that Germany was emerging not only as a great territorial power but as a naval power as well. In her search for colonies, the young empire collided with Britain everywhere—in South Africa, in North Africa, in the Pacific, in China. Germany's alliance with Austria-Hungary finally implied a move toward the Mediterranean and the British sphere in the Middle East, and her rapprochement with Turkey endangered the roads to India.

Typical British moves in the area of international relationships followed quickly. An agreement with Russia, out of the question only a few years before, was concluded in 1907. Where disputes over mutual interests were still unsettled—for instance, in Persia— a demarcation of Russian and British "spheres of influence" was resorted to in order to avoid further conflict. A British entente with France, settling colonial disputes, had been concluded as early as 1904. Everything was moving in the direction of a powerful anti-German coalition. Unity of purpose, this characteristic feature of British policy, was evident at every step.

The anti-German period in British policy was short —lasting less than two decades. It was, however, dramatic. It came to a climax during the first World War, when British Enemy Number One was again defeated and removed.

At the time of Germany's defeat in 1918 the earlier antagonist of Britain, Russia, following a military collapse and civil war, had ceased to play an important role in European politics, at least temporarily. The only important continental power at that time was

France. France possessed a large modern army and a great empire which rivaled Britain's at various points of the globe. She also possessed a navy which, although inferior to Britain's, was important enough to be reckoned with.

London had supported Germany in the latter's conflicts with France up to as recently as 1935 in order to create a check, a counterbalance, to the somewhat artificial French hegemony in the Old World. However, this was not the France of Louis XIV and of Napoleon. France's successes in the twentieth century did not spell mortal danger for Britain. Although France became the main antagonist of Britain in Western Europe after 1918, no war menace was involved in British-French relations during the interwar period.

Proof that French supremacy would be only temporary was the growing force of both Germany and Russia. Soviet Russia during the interwar period resumed her habitual moves toward Central Asia and the Far East. The movement now proceeded under cover of new ideas supplemented by the formula of "independence of backward nations." To Britain, however, the slogans mattered little. Russia was reverting to her old policy of expansionism. Soviet activity in China and the emergence of Chinese Communist armies were already, in the '30's, a problem for Britain. Soviet activity in the Middle East was the cause of numerous disputes between Moscow and London. The Middle East—Iraq, Iran, and Afghanistan—territories traditionally dominated by Britain, acquired new importance. British Governments which had been nervously apprehensive toward foreign penetration of this region during the nineteenth century became even more watchful in the twentieth, when this part of the world, formerly mere "pre-Indian territory," was being knit together and becoming increasingly important to the empire.

While the "Russian danger" to the empire was once more threatening, a new Germany, more vigorous than before, was also rising. Germany, considered merely as a countercheck against growing Russia, could be advantageous to Britain; but viewed as a world imperialist power, Germany was an enemy.

Both concepts had advocates in Chamberlain and Churchill. Both applied British standards and purely British means to achieve British aims: Chamberlain represented the century-old anti-Russian tradition. He was the promoter of the balance of power in Europe and "proud isolation." Churchill represented the tradition of interference in continental affairs when a dominance of one power over the whole of Europe was threatening.

Both the Chamberlain and Churchill concepts were logical. For immediate purposes Churchill's concept was more appropriate and he therefore ultimately won. The main question raised by Chamberlain, however, remained unanswered: what dangers will arise for Britain in Europe, in the Middle East, and in the Far East if Germany is defeated at the hands of mighty Russia? The issue was not dead when the war on Germany was declared; its determination was merely postponed.

Britain suppressed her anti-Russian tendencies to concentrate her force against Germany except for the duration of the Soviet-German agreement of 1939. A new anti-German period in British policy began in 1935 and has continued until 1945.

PRINCIPAL LINES OF POLICY

FROM this short survey the principal lines of British policy in Europe become obvious. Her successive campaigns against Spain, France, Russia, and Germany, and again against Russia and again against Germany, lasting for decades or centuries, in their continuity reveal the essential causes of her alliances, enmities, and wars during each period of her history. The object of these alliances and wars has been without exception attacks against the strongest continental power. Connected with this main objective have been certain rules of political conduct which have been followed by Britain and which may result in important developments within the next few years:

1. The Mediterranean is the traditional life line to the East. Unable to make of the Mediterranean an inner sea, a *mare nostrum*, Britain is watchful lest another great power become sufficiently powerful to endanger this life line. Of greatest importance is the eastern shore of the Mediterranean.

The political geography of the Mediterranean presents an amazing picture of British achievement. The entrance to the sea is dominated by "The Rock"—Gibraltar—the only British possession on the continent. The exit from the sea, the Suez Canal, also practically belongs to Britain. Halfway between Gibraltar and Suez lies the island of Malta, transformed by Britain into a first-class fortress and air base. The strategic importance of Malta was again demonstrated in 1942–43. Another island, Cyprus, defends the approaches to the Suez Canal and the mandated territories.

On the European shore of the Mediterranean Britain succeeded, after a long series of wars, first, in reducing Turkey to a small and powerless state, and, second, in sometimes securing Turkish collaboration by playing on the Turkish fear of Russia. Not feeling absolutely sure about Turkey, Britain helped to create modern Greece—a nation so strongly attached to Britain by reason of the rivalries in the Mediterranean and in the Balkans, that it may be considered in a sense as a strategical component of the empire, and certainly as a British base in time of war.

On the other side of the Mediterranean, Egypt, whose separation from Turkey was Britain's work, constitutes a part of the British sphere. The neighboring Italian possessions, which became a menace to Egypt in 1941–42, will in any event cease to be a threat to the Empire.

Finally, Italy's sea power was crushed during the second World War. For a long time to come Italy will not be able to oppose Britain in the Mediterranean.

2. The Balkans and the Dardanelles are a part of

the problem of the Eastern Mediterranean and Middle Asia. Gradual emancipation of the Balkan nations from the Turkish yoke in the nineteenth century has led to the creation of several independent states, all of which are small, militarily weak, and have no sea power. The liberation of the Balkan peoples was achieved chiefly by means of Russian arms and by liberal intervention from the west. But the "Balkanization" of the Balkans was a system which in this part of the world, where the interests of Russia, Austria, and Italy met, best suited British interests. Greece, as we have seen, was closely tied to Britain. Serbia and Montenegro (later Yugoslavia), Bulgaria, and Rumania constituted a sphere of Austro-Russian rivalry and because of this rivalry between the Big Ones the small nations were able to retain their independence. They constituted a sort of barrier to a further penetration of the Mediterranean area by two great Eastern European powers.

Britain, for instance, during the nineteenth and twentieth centuries, considered that it would be dangerous if Austria-Hungary annexed Serbia or Bulgaria. She looked even more askance at a Russian penetration into the Balkans, since the existence of a Russian port in this region would lead to the emergence of Russian naval forces in the Mediterranean. The best solution, so far as Britain was concerned, of the Balkan problem was exactly the system—or rather the chaos —that existed in relation to the Balkans for sixty years prior to 1938. Internal wars within the Balkans, shifting of frontiers, unification of small nations, and parceling of states did not affect British interests, so long as the great powers stayed out of the Balkans.

The British attitude on the question of the Dardanelles was a similar one. The Russian attempt during the nineteenth century to conquer this outlet from the Black Sea to the Mediterranean was unsuccessful largely because of the strong opposition of Britain. The world would have been much more complicated for Britain had Russia appeared in the Eastern Mediterranean with a navy of great battleships and cruisers.

During the first World War the British Government had to acquiesce in Russian demands regarding the Dardanelles, since it needed Russia as an ally against Germany and Turkey. What turn Russo-British relations would have taken had this program been realized is open to conjecture. But Russia herself renounced the Dardanelles treaty when the Revolution in Russia developed; and when Russia quit the war and concluded the Brest-Litovsk Treaty early in 1918, the question of Russian demands for the Dardanelles ceased to exist. Only this rejection of the old program made possible good relations between the Soviet and Turkey for two decades until 1939.

In September, 1939, however, the Soviet Government resumed its move to the south, and, using the new terminology, asked Turkey for "military bases" only. Backed by Britain, Turkey refused. Since that time Russo-Turkish relations have deteriorated. During the period 1941–44 Britain has taken pains to improve them but has met with only partial success. Because of this state of affairs, Turkey has since 1939 allied herself with Britain rather than with Russia.

3. A third maxim of British policy in Europe has been the support and creation of small nations, particularly from territories along the Atlantic coast. Norway, Denmark, Holland, Belgium, and Portugal constitute a British line of defense against the big powers. The union of the Netherlands with Belgium took place in 1815 because of the insistence of Britain, which needed the Netherlands as a buffer against continental powers. Fifteen years later Belgium, too, with British assistance, emerged as an independent nation. Portugal has for centuries been an ally of Britain.

This policy of protection of the small powers bordering on the Atlantic, coupled with an analogous policy in the Balkans, has given Britain the character of champion of the rights of small nations. It would be hypocrisy to assert that this policy of championing the small nations was inspired by moral principles held by the English nation. In the policies which she has applied in various territories throughout the world— for example, South Africa, Egypt, Burma—Britain has disclosed a tendency to conquest and an ability to carry out a program of national oppression when she deemed these necessary or useful. Europe, however, is a continent of a special kind. There is no territory in Europe which could be occupied and firmly held by British forces. Because the industrial level of the European nations is high, and because of inevitable conflicts with other great powers and the certain defeat of Britain were she to try to expand on the continent of Europe, her policy of supporting the small nations of this continent is the only sensible one. The small nations have served as Britain's weights on the scales of international balance of power.

This complicated yet consistent system of foreign policy is the consequence of Britain's situation in relation to the European continent. Any other non-European power would have had to adopt basically the same attitude toward Europe, which would imply contraction of Germany, balancing European powers against one another, and support of small nations. To an even greater degree this applies to the United States, Britain's ally and successor.

America has had no systematic policy in Europe. American participation in European affairs has been recent and has never been more than sporadic. As far as Europe is concerned there has been no continuity of action in Washington. Active interference in European affairs—with tanks, guns, and aviation— has been followed by a period of aloofness, activity alternated with passivity, sacrifices in blood with indifference, intervention with isolationism. This is the opposite of the picture of British relations to Europe.

A certain similarity does exist, however, in the relations of the two powers to the continent of Europe, not so much in policy as in basic interests. The political situation of Great Britain has been affected, first, by the existence of a channel separating England from Europe; second, by the political force and military potentialities of the European nations; third, by British fear of a Europe dominated by one great power; and fourth, by the radiations of continental European politics encountered by Britain in every part of the world.

At the time the British system was formed, during Britain's conflicts with mighty France in the seventeenth and eighteenth centuries, London was remote from the continental theater of wars and peaces. The shortest distance from London to a continental capital in those times took no less than two days to traverse. In order to land a small British army on the continent, a huge fleet of small wooden sailing ships was necessary. It took days to transmit political information of the highest importance from Paris to London.

In these respects America is nearer to Europe today than Britain was at that time. America is separated from Europe by an ocean which can be crossed in ten hours; large armies can be transferred from America to Europe more quickly than could British armies during the eighteenth century; communication between Europe and Washington requires a few minutes to establish. This comparison of the situation of the America of today with the situation of eighteenth-century Britain is of primary international importance. An analogy has emerged between the fundamental political attitudes of these two powers toward Europe—a similarity which has made possible the association in war between them in 1917–18 and in 1941–45. America, not unlike Britain, is menaced only when a European power threatens to assume all-European hegemony; America encounters European influence in other parts of the world and opposes it; America is interested, as is Britain, in the independent existence of small and medium-sized European nations. And America appears to Europe, just as Britain appeared in the nineteenth century, as a fabulously rich, shrewd, omnipotent force, always able to achieve its goal whether by paying for it in gold or by fighting for it.

This is why for a long time America could be satisfied with Britain's handling of European affairs. Criticizing, condemning, and sometimes hating British Governments, America actually lived in freedom and acquired wealth and power because Britain has been guided in her activities in Europe by interests not unlike her own.[12] America enjoyed the luxury of passivity because of Britain's activity.

12. If Britain were to be defeated, "the British Navy would no longer be able to prevent a German expansion across the Atlantic. The United States would lose one of the basic elements in its present national security . . . British seapower plays a decisive role in the Eastern Atlantic, setting a definite limit to the westward activities of any continental fleet or combination of fleets. The virtual guarantee of our Atlantic security by Great Britain is, of course, entirely involuntary, but, since it is based upon self-interest, it is none the less effective." Livingston Harley, in the *North American Review*, Spring, 1938.

Facing the Continent of Europe

This state of affairs began to change in 1917, and since 1941 the old relationship has been no longer in effect. American policy in Europe is necessarily bound to travel more or less along the same road as British policy in the past. Because England is in Europe, she will have to act in future, as has been the case in late years, on behalf of both herself and the United States on that continent. She will actually be the European agent of the two policies. The process of adjustment between the two policies cannot, of course, be smooth and without friction. Conflicts are bound to occur in the future, as they have occurred on several occasions during the war, before a perfect coördination can be achieved. Essentially, however, rapprochement between the two policies is already far advanced. America, her face turned toward Europe, is incorporating in her system most of Britain's continental policies.

V

OBJECTIVES AND AIMS OF SOVIET POLICY

THE use of military terms in nonmilitary, even nonpolitical matters, has crept into our common language in the last thirty martial years. In no country in the world, however, is military terminology as widely used as in Russia. "On the scientific *front* this year there has been success," they say. There exist in Russia the "industrial *front*," the "health *front*," "ideological *fronts*." "Our *offensive* against typhus is progressing," they say. "The *fortress* of illiteracy was taken by *storm*." "The *battle* for a new waterpipe has been won." "Pavlov was a great *fighter* for a new biology." And so on.

The general use of military terms indicates a military trend of thought. The concept of a gigantic war that has been going on incessantly since November, 1917, colors the thinking as well as the new way of expressing this thinking. The concept is one of a conflict of enormous proportions representing the outstanding event of recent history, a conflict that does not cease with the signing of armistices and peace treaties; a war between capitalism and Communism. The belief in this concept, far from being dead, has, on the contrary, been strengthened by the events of recent years. This belief animates, inspires, and implements a policy which otherwise would appear as an inexplicable sequence of undirected moves.

Before 1917, according to this concept, a political struggle of parties and classes was going on in different countries; the period before 1917 was, in a way, a preparatory one. Since November, 1917, however, the political struggle has become a war, with all the features of a war, with its own strategical system, with enormous and bloody sacrifices, and with everyday politics subordinated to the supreme goal.

The Great Social War, in the Soviet view, has been going on since 1917, but its strategy, like war strategy in general, is subject to change with circumstances: there was one strategy when the Allies landed in North Africa, and quite another when they reached the Siegfried Line. One Russian strategy prevailed when the German armies were rushing toward the Volga; a different strategy was applied by Soviet troops in Prussia.

The concept views world capitalism as a fortress— a vast stronghold occupying a tremendous area—a fortress almost impregnable. It is besieged by an army of anticapitalism, strong in numbers and strong in hatred, but with almost no means at hand of blasting the walls of the fortress. Frontal attacks and assaults one after another occurred before 1917—in 1848, in 1870, in 1905—but they were repulsed with enormous losses. The concrete walls remained unshaken. In 1917, for the first time in history, the assault met with success. The cost was high; millions perished. But at one spot the walls of capitalism were broken, and one of its seventy towers, the Russian tower, was occupied by a detachment of the besieging army. After a few years—the years of the civil war—it became obvious that this tower of the great fortress had been finally lost to capitalism and would be firmly held by the insurgent army.

The breakthrough was accomplished at one spot only. What would be the next strategical move? Must the besieging armies wage their war in the old manner, by frontal assaults against the fortress of steel and concrete in order to achieve a second, a third, a tenth, and a fiftieth breakthrough and, pouring in from outside, occupy one tower after another—the German, the French, the British, etc.—until all the strong points of capitalism fall to the besieging armies of Communism?

No, says Moscow. This would be a mistake. The army which has succeeded in penetrating the fortress has special tasks to perform; it would not fulfil its duties if it did not give assistance to troops still outside the walls. The tower occupied by the insurgents is surrounded by scores of other strong towers. If these were to unite in one military bloc, they would, of course, be able to eject the intruding revolutionists from the fortress and restore the *status quo ante* 1917. The insurgents, therefore, must by every means hold fast to their conquest. They must act shrewdly and cautiously. They must at times cease open fighting and conclude peace treaties with their neighbor forts. They must participate in internal conflicts within the fortress if this should be necessary in order to prevent a united front on the part of the hostile positions. But they must remember (and they do remember, Stalin insisted, on the eve of the second World War) that their fate is indissolubly tied to that of the armies on the outside engaged in besieging the huge fortress. Occupation of one of the towers cannot be lasting: if other towers do not fall to the insurgent forces, the one isolated tower will sooner or later be destroyed.

The new policy, far from being treacherous to Leninism, is actually the application of the principles of Leninism to an entirely new situation. Between 1919 and 1924 the "outside armies" tried to wage their war in the old manner. The results were unsuccessful. The insurrections in Hungary, Bavaria, Saxony, Estonia were costly and futile, because the Soviet Union was not in a position to lend them any real assistance. Therefore the strategy had to be reformed.

Further victories depend on the successes of the Russian fort: its strengthening will open the gates to the insurgent forces outside the walls. These forces do not hold the initiative; they must wait until activity within the fortress has caused the walls to yield in new places.

The old Soviet plan may be said to have embraced concepts of an *extensive* revolution, or rather of a series of revolutions: extensive because it was expected that all over the globe irregular, chaotic explosions would occur; today Germany, tomorrow perhaps Norway, then America or Japan. These explosions were not expected to be confined to one geographical center; the soil of the whole globe was considered to be volcanic; in a hundred places the revolutionary lava would break through the crust. Lenin died before this concept was abandoned; Trotsky adhered to it to the end.

What Stalin has done with the old concept has not been to abolish the revolutionary program; rather he has transformed the idea of an extensive revolution into one of an *intensive* revolution. Of course, the old system of capitalist economy and capitalist policy, he said, is everywhere ripe for destruction, but the forces of the governing classes are so strong that extensive eruptions have only small chance of succeeding. Only through combination with the first great stronghold of Communism—Russia—can upheavals and movements be successful. But Russia can give assistance chiefly to its neighbor peoples. It is easier for Russia to lend a hand in Poland than in Brazil. The defeat of the Loyalists in the Spanish Civil War was indirect proof that the geographical scheme had to be revised: now the progress of Communism would be parallel to the expansion of the sphere of Soviet influence. Again the analogy to a real war and to the towers of a fortress became alive: the forts neighboring the occupied tower can more easily be transformed through infiltration, military or diplomatic, than by the use of old-fashioned battering rams smashing at the walls from outside.

The most striking example of what this reversal of

concepts has meant was supplied by the Chinese Communist movement. In the early '30's several territories in southeastern China, far from the Soviet frontier, were occupied by the Chinese Red Armies and were constituted as Soviet states; their capital was Juichin, in Kiangsi province. The Chiang Kai-shek government waged a war against them, which, however, did not succeed in annihilating the Red armies. In 1934, however, the forces of the Nationalist Government became overwhelming and the defeat of the Red Armies appeared inevitable. It was resolved then to move the Chinese Soviet Government and the Red Armies to other provinces, in the immediate vicinity of Russia. Since 1935 the northern Border Region has become the center of the Soviet state, its capital in Yenan, near the Chinese wall at the border of Mongolia nearer to the Soviet sphere. It is as if Soviet China survived through being transplanted onto Soviet Russia.

THE "INTENSIVE" REVOLUTION

THE first inference to be drawn from the new scheme is that there has been a seeming reversal of Soviet policy back to the paths of the old imperialism. In the days of the empire it was an accepted idea that expansion of territory was the road to greatness; the necessity of aggrandizement—in the west, south, and east—was not questioned; only the feasibility had to be weighed. The idea of a national state on the lines of the French, Italian, or Spanish state was never accepted by Imperial Russia. From of old, Russia has been a multinational state and it continued to expand along this road, annexing Finns in Finland, Rumanians in Bessarabia, Poles in Poland, Tatars, Georgians, and Armenians in the Caucasus, and a multitude of other nations in Asia. The old empire did not recognize the danger inherent in conquest and annexation of alien nationalities, and to the very end did not admit that, for instance, the part of Poland incorporated into Russia was actually a source of weakness to the Empire rather than an addition to its greatness.

Already a colossus, old Russia still nourished ideas of new expansion. A successful war was one that fulfilled a program of territorial aggrandizement. Plans were ripening for the extension of Russia's might to territories adjoining the empire: Austrian Galicia and Ruthenia, German East Prussia, the Dardanelles, and a number of Turkish vilayets in Asia Minor, northern Iran, the northern provinces of China, Manchuria, and Korea in the Far East. In certain cases—in regard to Iran and the Far East, for instance—programs were concrete and exact. In other instances, territories— particularly those belonging to Austria and Turkey —were already awarded to Russia under international treaties which, however, did not materialize because of the outbreak of the revolution.

The new Soviet concept of *intensive* development necessitates the assumption of certain of the features of the old imperial policy. Reference to former imperial policy is now considered a valuable diplomatic asset. Expansion of any kind is a difficult job; occupation of a country by armed forces is only half of it. Resistance on the part of the outside world, particularly of the great powers, must be broken—not by military but by diplomatic means. The old imperial rights, privileges, treaties, therefore suddenly assume a practical significance. They can serve as a basis for demands. "You, our allies, were willing to cede to old Russian Governments the whole of Poland, half of Austria, slices of Turkey, and other lands. How can you now object if the present Russian Government claims the right to the same territories?"

The intensive concept of revolution, coupled with restoration of former Russian privileges and acquired rights, means that five different territorial zones surrounding Russia are becoming objects of her policy.

First, there are the integral parts of old Russia, whose return to the Soviet Union would be comparatively easy to justify. Bessarabia and the Baltic States fall in this category, as does a strip of present Turkish territory (the Kars region, south of the Caucasus). Of course, no vote was taken in the Baltic countries or Bessarabia, nor will there be voting in future cases.

Second, there are the former Russian "spheres of influence" which would have to be returned to the control of Moscow. Chief among these are northern Persia and Manchuria, and, less important, Korea. Finland, which was an autonomous Grand Duchy under the empire, belongs in this category.

Third, there are the territories which, although they

77

were never under the control of the Empire, were designed by treaties or otherwise to become annexed to it: northern Bukovina, eastern Czechoslovakia, eastern Galicia, East Prussia, the Dardanelles, and Turkish Armenia. Poland, viewed as an autonomous component of the future Russia during the first World War, also belongs to this group.

Fourth, there is the outer ring of territory surrounding the lands already mentioned, which would automatically become a Russian sphere of influence if the first parts of the territorial program are realized. This consists of the whole of Bohemia, Slovakia, Hungary, Rumania, Austria, Yugoslavia, Bulgaria; in Asia, Sinkiang and northern China.

Fifth, there are the lands and peoples outside the ring of territory surrounding Russia. In certain cases religious factors may serve as a means of intensive development; for instance, the Orthodox Church in Greece, and Mohammedanism in the Arab and Indian world. In other cases "anti-fascist" sentiments may be used, as for instance in northern China. In the most important of all cases, that of Germany, retribution for the war may serve as a reason for the extension of Russian influence to at least eastern and northern Germany and for the remolding of Germany's political and social system.

Northern Bukovina is a small territory of no great importance in European politics. The manner in which the Soviet Union acquired it, however, was an example of the new trend of thought and of the course of policy now being pursued by Moscow.

In June, 1940, the Soviet Government presented an ultimatum to Rumania calling for immediate cession of Bessarabia, which had been part of Russia until 1918 and had been included in the Soviet "sphere of interests" by the Soviet-German pacts of August–September, 1939. Along with Bessarabia Moscow also demanded northern Bukovina. This was quite unexpected. Bukovina had never belonged to the empire, nor was it mentioned in the Soviet-German treaties. When Foreign Commissar Molotov was called upon to explain this demand in his ultimatum to Rumania, he did it clumsily. He presented the annexation as a kind of rent to be paid by Rumania for a two-decade lease of Bessarabia. The cession of northern Bukovina, he wrote, "would compensate . . . for the great wrong done to the Soviet Union and to the population of Bessarabia by the twenty-two years of Rumanian domination of Bessarabia." It was a strange argument in international affairs.

The truth of the matter was that the Russian claims to northern Bukovina were supported by the powers in 1914–15. At that time the whole of Bukovina formed part of Austria. Russia was at war with Austria and, in agreement with France and Britain, strove to bring Rumania into the war on the side of the Allies. Their negotiations considered annexation of different territories of Austria-Hungary by Rumania, provided

79

Rumania would join the war; as far as Bukovina was concerned, the Allies proposed a division, Rumania to obtain the southern part (populated mainly by Rumanians) and Russia to annex the north (with Slavs predominating). The Rumanian Government, however, claimed almost the whole of Bukovina and, in the end, got it.

In 1940 Russia took from Rumania what the powers were ready to concede to her a quarter of a century ago. Since Lenin's government had declared all such rights to annexations void, it was not possible publicly to base the Soviet demands on prerevolutionary diplomatic negotiations. Molotov, therefore, had to resort to lame argumentation.

Another development of the same kind, of far greater importance, took place in 1944–45 in the relations between the Soviet Government and Czechoslovakia concerning the territory of Carpatho-Ruthenia and eastern Slovakia. These lands, Austrian before 1918, were firmly included in the Russian annexation plans of 1914–16. When Czechoslovakia emerged as an independent state after the armistice of 1918, she included Carpatho-Ruthenia. This development has never been opposed or disputed by Moscow. In the wartime agreements concluded between the Soviet and the Beneš government (1943), the underlying idea was the restoration to Czechoslovakia of her territorial integrity; moreover, the Beneš government was the most friendly toward Moscow of all the allied governments, because of its hope that by submission to its mighty neighbor it would gain territorial integrity and security.

At the end of 1944 the Red Army drove the German troops out of Carpatho-Ruthenia. In accordance with the treaties, the Beneš government was now to take over the management of civilian affairs in the liberated areas. But when the Czech emissaries arrived, they found that the Ruthenian Communist party (which could scarcely act against the wishes of Moscow) was demanding Soviet annexation of eastern Czechoslovakia. A plebiscite had even been held, they were informed, which resulted in the expected victory of the pro-Russian program. Moscow was silently saying, "You Czechoslovaks profited in 1918 by the weakness of Soviet Russia; these lands would not belong to you had not Russia been defeated by Germany in 1917–18; now you must turn them over to the Soviet Union." Since a statement couched in such language is, naturally, inconceivable, so-called ballotings and plebiscites had to take place. In April, 1945, when the Beneš government returned from London, via Moscow, to Czechoslovakia, the new Premier, Zdenek Fierlinger, had to announce the "new foreign policy" of his nation and promise the settlement of the "Carpatho-Ukrainian question in accordance with the wishes of the Ukrainian population," meaning the annexation of the territory to the Ukrainian Soviet Republic, member of the USSR.

UNEXPLORED MOUNTAINS

In outward appearance the scheme of intensive revolution at most points resembles the old imperialist program. It deliberately derives certain claims and demands from the ancient dreams of Russian expansion. As far as underlying ideas are concerned, however, the program is essentially different. Even larger in scope than the program of old Russia, the scheme implies that the lands and nations which fall into the Soviet sphere will be ruled by a government of the same nationality, which is alleged to be sufficient and decisive proof that they will be really independent. For the outside world the outstanding fact is the virtual appointment by the Soviet Union of the governments which are to rule these lands. According to the Soviet concept, however, these governments are representatives of their peoples, only sharing the basic political and social ideas prevailing in the Soviet Union. They are not the voice of the majority of these peoples? What of it? Moscow asks. The Soviet Government, when it came to power, did not even pretend to have the support of the majority. Lenin referred to his régime as dictatorial. Nevertheless it has become, as this concept sees it, the most progressive regime in the world. Why should not a similar development be expected to occur in the other countries which as a result of the war have come under Soviet influence, but which are to be called "great and independent"?

Stalin has often been depicted as an extremely wily

individual; astuteness has been said to be the main characteristic of his personality. But it is not only Stalin's personal traits that lend Soviet policy its character of cunning and shrewdness. Rather the requirements of grand strategy make the use of adroitness as a political weapon imperative.

A forthright and open government policy is appropriate when a concrete and limited objective has been set. To propose abolition of slavery or to advocate its continuance, to accept the New Deal or to abolish it —in these and in hundreds of similar cases no shrewdness is necessary; the best policy is the direct policy. But if the goals are far reaching and complicated, if their achievement involves a multitude of various interests, if the direct roads are barred by superior forces, if there is a readiness to engage in a hard and long struggle, then means other than the direct and forthright must be resorted to. A superior force can employ frontal attacks, but the inferior force is compelled to choose circuitous means. To raise weak Germany to the rank of an overwhelming military power, Adolf Hitler built up a labyrinth of international deceit, starting with the Reichstag fire. He concocted "Soviet fliers in the German skies" to justify the building of a huge Luftwaffe. After each territorial annexation he gave his *Ehrenwort* that this was the last—only to break the promise on the very next occasion. When finally confronted with his lies and hypocrisy, he exclaimed: "I did it for Germany!"

The goals set by Soviet leadership are certainly far

reaching. They meet with the greatest of obstacles. The strategy therefore makes shrewdness imperative. In 1920 Lenin wrote, "We have to use any ruse, dodges, tricks, cunning, unlawful method, concealment, veiling of truth." [1] Many of his followers demurred at his sly tactics, his "zigzagging and maneuvering," his compromising with the enemy. He answered them: "Suppose we have to ascend an unexplored and, so far, impregnable mountain, would we decline to go, at times, in a zigzag course, now and then to return, to renounce the direction previously chosen by us and to try various directions?" When accused of slandering his factional adversaries, he outlined his ideas of sportsmanship before a party tribunal. When fighting his foes, he said, even if they were personally honest, he nevertheless deliberately chose terms and words "which are bound to provoke hatred and disgust toward these people, in order to annihilate and erase their organization. . . . The terms must provoke the worst suspicions about the enemy." (The enemy in this case was the other faction in his party). "We have learned diplomacy in our struggle with the Mensheviks," Lenin facetiously remarked when he was already head of the government. This was more than a joke. During the fourteen years of his struggle

1. *Infantile Sickness of "Leftism" in Communism.* In this pamphlet Lenin applied his political strategy to the question of how to gain access to American and British trade-unions which were barring Communists from membership. The principles were, of course, to be applied to a still greater degree in major issues of international policy.

with the other faction he made ruthless and adroit use of party statutes to win a majority in the congresses and committees and on the editorial boards, and many a trick served him in this fight. To a far greater degree Lenin's principles were applied by his successor and true disciple, Stalin. The enemies inside or outside the party were treated according to Lenin's precept: the worst suspicions are good "in order to annihilate and erase" them.

The same principle of using "ruse and concealment" was applied to diplomacy, which soon became the main field for its application. It was not because it was a hobby of Stalin's that the principle became important. During the war alliance of 1941–45 these methods were necessary if long-range aims, often contrary to the interests of the allies, were to be achieved.

One instance of the use of shrewd diplomacy was the playing up of Slavdom. Neither Stalin nor his party ever felt any racial preference for the Slav peoples of Central or Southern Europe; but the slogans were opportune and appropriate for penetration into this sphere and Russian sponsorship of Communist regimes. The sponsorship of the Orthodox Church was another move of the same kind. The slogans of Russian supernationalism and the anti-German racial formulas acquired particular importance; the underlying sentiments were accepted neither by Stalin nor by his party, but they served the immediate aims of its policy. The slogan of "friendly governments" in neighboring countries as a security measure for Russia was used to justify far-reaching interference in the internal affairs of the bordering lands. In the Middle East a demand for oil concessions was the cover for a political campaign that had no relation to oil. Foremost among the modern slogans was "democracy." Critics of democracy ("formal democracy is the program of the rich, dictatorship of the toilers is that of the peoples") declared themselves its strongest adherents, and it was now in the service of democracy that minority parties in Greece, Belgium, and other countries fought the majority of their peoples.

But oil concessions, nationalism, democracy, religious movements, anti-Germanism were more acceptable to public opinion among the allied nations than other underlying aims. Only under these disguises was Moscow's policy able to make headway in the presence of paradoxical war conditions and in the course of an alliance with the mightiest capitalist powers of the world.

THE SOVIET NAVY

THESE far-reaching goals of Soviet policy can be achieved only in competition with other powers and in the face of possible conflicts. Considerable military force is a precondition of successes. Therefore, real disarmament is out of the question; expansion of war industries becomes a necessity; aviation must be developed on a large scale. This alone, however, is not sufficient. A great navy, too, must be created, since naval power often plays a decisive role in competition among world powers.

Russia has never been a great naval power. Before the revolution she hardly participated in the competition of the naval nations. In 1914 the Russian Navy occupied seventh place among the world powers; compared with Britain's Navy, Russia's 280,000 tons were modest. Her shipbuilding facilities were limited to a few shipyards and plants; purchase of warships abroad was limited by the financial situation. Her main outlets to the sea, except in the Far East, could be barred either by foreign powers or by ice. Russia therefore remained a distinctly land power until the very end of the old regime.

From the beginning of the Soviet period until 1934 the navy attracted little attention in Russia. Having been destroyed during the war and postwar period, it was never rebuilt except for a few small units. The general situation became alarming when Germany's Navy in the Baltic assumed large proportions; in the Far East the Japanese Navy was a menace, too. The Soviet Government began to give a certain amount of attention to its navy. The idea was the construction of a purely "defensive navy." Even this limited aim involved a difficult task. "Comrade Stalin," Molotov reported in January, 1934, "has taken it up himself in the Stalin way, and I have no doubt that the navy will be strong." Two years later President Kalinin was still demanding that more attention be given to naval problems. "I would like to see the navy play a greater role.

The time has arrived for the navy to participate to a greater degree in the defense of the country."

A navy of defense—this was the slogan during that initial period, until 1937. The Soviet concept of a "navy of defense" implied first of all the construction of submarines, of a certain amount of other small-size vessels, and fortification of coasts at strategic spots. Creation of a navy of this kind required relatively small appropriations and was possible of achievement under the conditions of Soviet industry as they existed at the beginning of the second Five Year Plan. In the three years from 1934 through 1936 the number of submarines increased more than sevenfold. "We had to create and we have created," V. Orlov, Chief of the Navy, said in November, 1936, "a powerful *defensive* navy . . . the number of *small* surface craft, the defense of the shores, has grown threefold in that period."

In the meantime the Spanish Civil War had begun and immediately naval power attained great importance. Italy's intervention was made possible through her strong navy; the German Navy, too, played an important role. Soviet assistance to Spain was limited because of her naval weakness, and the course of events in Spain meant, as far as Soviet intervention was concerned, a naval defeat. It was clear to Moscow that the Soviet voice in the London Conferences of the powers was feeble because of her utter weakness as a sea power.

In 1937 a naval pact was concluded between Russia and Britain. Russia adhered to the main principles adopted in the Washington Conference of 1936 but remained free in the Far East, since Japan was not bound by the Washington agreements. As far as Europe was concerned, the Anglo-German naval agreements, too, were considered insufficient safeguards. In general, the Soviet Government considered the network of naval treaties unreal and inefficient.[2]

Is it true, it was asked now, that the Soviet state does not need a navy other than a defensive force of small vessels? If it is to enhance its importance in international affairs, submarines obviously are not sufficient. At the end of 1936 a new attitude emerged. "We must construct and we are building a really big navy, which includes vessels of all classes of the highest technical standing," was the comment of V. Orlov, following the decision of the Soviet Government.

The task was considerable. Three large warships of prerevolutionary design had to be rebuilt and this required the use of extensive technical facilities. The construction of great new warships was not yet possible. The suggestion was made to try to have them built in the United States. Sam Carp, a brother-in-law of the Soviet Premier, an American citizen and head of the Carp Corporation, began negotiations in New York for the construction of two 35,000-ton battleships. The negotiations fell through in spite of the fact that an outlay for the purpose of $100,000,000 had been authorized. The plans were rejected by the Soviet naval specialists.

2. Molotov's speech of January 15, 1938.

While military and especially naval leaders were still talking of a defensive sea force, and while writers on military affairs were still commenting favorably on the limited naval program, the highest leaders, with Stalin the first among them, took a new step in the rearmament program, a step of enormous significance. The land forces at that time adopted the formula: the Red Army, in case of a war, will have "to beat the enemy on his own territory" in order to save the Soviet land from devastation. Why not apply the same principle to the naval forces? The present fleet of submarines and small surface vessels, even with the assistance of a few cruisers, would be able at best to repel attacks by the navy of the enemy. Why not apply the formula of the Red Army to the Red Navy? In 1937–38 the leaders introduced the concept, "to transfer the war on sea to the waters of the enemy and there to beat him."

The sentiment for a big navy was growing. The sky was the limit. These were the successful years of the second Five Year Plan, when every week one or another industry reported victories in the race of production. Statistical figures appeared to be convincing: Europe was outflanked; Russia was becoming the greatest industrial nation in the old world.

A modern navy, it was argued, is a manifestation of the technical productive power of a nation. A great warship, with its machinery, radio, electrical apparatus, is an industrial city afloat, one of the most complicated products of science and labor. Old Russia, because of her economic backwardness, was not able to build up a great navy and to become a great naval power. But the Soviet Union had become, people in Moscow believed, one of the most powerful industrial countries in the world, and there were no obstacles to her development as a great naval power.

"The mighty Soviet power must possess," Molotov said, "a sea and ocean navy adequate for her interests and worthy of our great cause." These words were later repeated by everyone in the navy, from the People's Commissar down to the lecturer in the smallest sailors' group. A navy "worthy of our great cause" cannot be inferior to any other navy since the "cause" is greater than the cause of any capitalist nation. The conclusion was soon reached that the Soviet Union must possess the greatest and the finest navy in the world. It must be "second to none." Was this competition with the old ruler of the seas, Britain? Why not?

President Mikhail Kalinin made an important speech at a meeting of shipbuilding workers in Leningrad on July 2, 1938: "So far no one," he said, "has outdone England. We have to outdo her! England is the strongest capitalist country, we are the strongest socialist country!"

He enumerated the next tasks as follows:

"First, to build fast. The construction of a great navy cannot wait.

"Second, to build cheaply.

"Third, to build well: our vessels must be the best in the world."

"You enter a competition with the strongest capitalist powers—with England, the United States, Japan, France, Germany, Italy; each of the great powers has paid much attention to her navy.

"And we have to outdo these nations."

The official party organ commented on the new program: "For our country it is not sufficient to have a navy which is able to beat the enemy near the Soviet shores. [This was a clear-cut repudiation of the theory of a "navy for defense."] We must possess enough big warships together with plentiful light craft to annihilate the enemy, if he dares to attack us, in any sea, in any ocean." And, it concluded:

"The mighty Soviet power must have the strongest sea and ocean navy in the world. The Soviet ships must be the best in the world!" [3]

"The strongest navy in the world" has been the slogan since 1938. In that year the leading Russian naval publication declared: "The USSR, a mighty Socialist power, must have the strongest sea and ocean navy in the world: such is the will of the party and of the government, such is the will of the genius, Stalin." [4]

"We will possess the best ships, and they will travel farther and move faster than the ships of capitalist

3. *Partyinoye Stroitelstvo*, February, 1939.
4. *Morskoi Sbornik*, 1938, No. 2.

states. Stalin's policy is clear: we must have a strong navy." [5]

Stalin's decisive role in the framing of the new naval program was apparent; he was prodding his party and his collaborators. Prodding was necessary, since the new policy was in more than one respect a reversal of the theories which prevailed during the first two decades of the Soviet regime. It was not easy to turn the political course in this direction; a far-reaching purge was applied to eliminate from the navy all those who hesitated and who doubted whether the new tasks could be fulfilled.

All the leading personalities of the Red Navy had previously adhered to the concept of a comparatively small "navy of defense." Rivalry with Britain on the seas was not only impossible, in their view, but unnecessary, costly, and imperialistic. The slogan of a "peace policy," at that time propagated by Litvinov and his Foreign Office, was taken too seriously by these people. "Defense of the Soviet fatherland," in their view, was a matter of pure defense, with no dreams of spheres of influence, security zones,.and expansion. "Supremacy on the seas" was no aim of Soviet policy, as many saw it. They were in more than one respect akin to the Right Opposition, which had practically ceased to expect a catastrophe for the great capitalist powers in the near future. From their knowledge of the navy and of Soviet shipbuilding facilities, they had come to the conclusion that naval supremacy could

5. Kuznetsov, at the Eighteenth Party Congress, 1939.

not be achieved. The flower of naval leadership belonged to this school of thought. When the government embarked on its great naval program, this group had to be liquidated. Its ideas of a small navy were now presented to the Soviet people as a program of the enemy and its adherents as agents of foreign powers. The Soviet press listed as agents of fascism, who "have done all they could to hamper the development of our navy," the following: Admiral Orlov, Chief of the Navy; Romuald Muklevich; Alexander Sivkov, Chief of the Baltic Fleet; Ivan Ludri, Assistant Chief of the Soviet Navy; Chief of the Black Sea Navy Kozhanov; Director of the Naval Academy Stasevich and Professor Alexandrov; and others. Along with them a number of minor officers were liquidated, too. Crimes against the Big Navy program were charged also to Marshal Mikhail Tukhachevski. Although not a navy man, he had fought, according to the official reports, against naval expansion in his capacity as a leader of the Soviet armed forces.

People's Commissar Tevosyan reported later that "the enemies of the people, the agents of fascism, Tukhachevski, Orlov, Muklevich, and other loathsome fascists, tried to demonstrate that we do not need a powerful surface navy; they have done much in order to prevent the addition to the navy of new surface warships." [6] (This was an exaggeration, since no one of the named military leaders opposed the building of surface vessels; the real issue was the size of the fu-

6. Speech at the Eighteenth Congress, 1939.

ture navy and the international implications of a Soviet Navy "second to none.")

The new Chief of the Baltic Navy, Tributs, wrote that the "unmasked people's enemies, Ludri and Alexandrov, conducted a struggle with the party; they tried to prove that our country does not need a great navy." [7] "The Orlovs, Muklevichs, Sivkovs, Ludris, and their like are destroyed; with their twaddle about the possibility or impossibility of supremacy on the seas they tried to prevent the addition to the navy of new surface ships." [8]

The new personnel of the navy, succeeding the liquidated leaders, did everything possible, and almost the impossible, to avoid a similar fate. Construction of the Big Navy was pushed; it became a political campaign. Navy Day, introduced in July, 1938, had to be celebrated every year by large meetings, lectures, and by the general press. Until 1938 the navy had been a part of the Defense Commissariat; in that year a special People's Commissariat was created for it. In addition, in 1939 a special Commissariat for Shipbuilding was created. The term of active service in the navy was raised from four to five years. Andrei Zhdanov, Stalin's right-hand man, was appointed a member of the Supreme Naval Council. Twenty thousand members of the Communist Youth League were taken into the navy. Ninety-four per cent of the students in the naval schools were league members. Even among the sailors

7. *Morskoi Sbornik*, 1939, No. 12.
8. *Ibid.*

17 per cent were party members and 50 per cent were Comsomols. The combined percentage of party members in the naval personnel—67 per cent—was higher than in the Red Army.

Shipbuilding was pushed with utmost energy, since it was known that Stalin personally was directing the effort. There was "not a single plan of a naval vessel, of a naval gun, of a great or small problem in general, which did not pass through the hands of Comrade Stalin," reported Tevosyan in 1939. The main task was acceleration of the shipbuilding program, since "the Soviet plants are behind the foreign ones, especially the English. Everything must be subordinated to the task of accelerated shipbuilding." The third Five Year Plan (whose details have never been revealed) provided for enormous sums for the naval program; the idea was expressed by *Izvestiya* (July 24, 1939): "In the next years the USSR will occupy one of the first places in the production of vessels, both in number and tonnage."

"By 1942 the Soviet shipyards will win one of the world's first places in annual production of tonnage," declared Kosienko, Commissar of Shipbuilding, in July, 1940. The publication *Na Strazhe* reported at the same time that the Soviet Government had started "construction of vessels equal to those of any foreign power."

Military shipbuilding activities, cloaked in deepest secrecy, were showing really good results only as far as the relatively easier task was concerned, namely, the building of submarines and small surface vessels. In 1939 Russia possessed more submarines than any other power; more than Germany and Japan combined.[9] In 1940 three times as many new submarines were added to the navy as in 1939.

As far as big vessels were concerned, however, progress was unsatisfactory. The three old battleships of pre-1914 design were rebuilt and renovated; a certain number of medium-sized vessels were in process of construction. Plans had been completed for three big battleships of 36,000 tons each and, according to reports in the world press, one of them was actually built. Four new destroyers and two aircraft carriers were also started in Leningrad before the war. No reliable information as to progress in construction was available. In June, 1941, *Izvestiya* reported that a big warship had slid down the ways. No information was revealed as to either the class of vessel or the place from which it was launched. "Very little reliable information is obtainable about the Soviet Navy," reported the authoritative *Jane's Fighting Ships*, in 1940, "but everything goes to suggest that shipbuilding still proceeds at a very slow rate." "The proposed reconstruction proceeds slowly," reported the *Statesman's Yearbook* in 1941.

The government tried to buy big warships abroad. In 1939 a Soviet naval commission visited America with the aim of opening negotiations through the

9. Report of People's Commissar of the Navy Kuznetsov, July 23, 1939.

Carp Corporation with American firms as well as with the State Department. The American Government reversed its negative attitude toward Soviet purchases of naval units in the United States and, probably in view of the situation in the Far East, was ready to approve the proposed commercial deals. However, no practical results materialized from these negotiations up to the time the European war started. The Russian-German agreement put an end to these plans. Then Germany undertook to deliver a certain amount of naval material to Russia and to assist in expanding her navy.

In the war with Germany, Russia had to fight only a section of the German Navy in the Baltic and in the Black Sea. The grouping of world powers—with Russia on the side of Britain—appeared to confirm the concepts of the liquidated leaders of the navy: sea supremacy was neither possible nor necessary.

New naval construction naturally almost ceased in Russia during the war years; this was an important point of difference between the Russian situation and that of America and Britain. While the latter two nations were becoming stronger on the seas, Russia was not able to make good her naval losses.

The Soviet Government claimed one third of the Italian Navy; in lieu thereof it obtained certain units which were transferred to Russia by the United States and Britain in 1943 and 1944. The British battleship *Royal Sovereign*, renamed the *Archangelsk*, is a fine, large vessel of 29,000 tons. The American cruiser

Milwaukee has likewise been added to the Red Navy and renamed the *Murmansk*. The Soviet Navy will probably inherit a part of the German Navy. Eleven naval colleges are already operating, among them five for the Baltic navy, one for the Black Sea, one for the Caspian, and two for the Pacific. While buying commercial vessels abroad, the Soviet will be able to start military shipbuilding at its old shipyards as well as at those which fall in its sphere: In Königsberg, Stettin, Riga, and Finland.

The concept of a big Soviet Navy is by no means dead. The idea of a navy as a prerequisite to a successful world policy took deep root in the Soviet Government during the last five years preceding the war. Neither Germany nor Japan will constitute a menace to Russia in the postwar period, but Russia will meet Britain and America at every step in Europe and Asia. There cannot be any doubt that among the first objectives of the postwar period the rehabilitation and construction of a powerful Soviet Navy will occupy a prominent place.

OUTLET TO THE OCEANS

THE program of a big Russian Navy involves the solution of another old question of Russian great navy policy—that of an outlet to the oceans. A part of the navy can and will remain in the Far East. But the distance from the Pacific to the main scenes of European politics is too great. The question of outlets to the sea is bound once more to become acute.

The port of Murmansk (2 on the map on p. 101) is the only port in northern Russia which is free of ice. However, its location in the far north, seven hundred miles from Leningrad, in a thinly populated region and close to a foreign frontier, makes it unsuitable as a main base for a great navy. Before the revolution the Russian Government was discussing plans for building a railroad across Finland to the Norwegian port of Narvik (3 on the map); the plans were dropped. Apart from the huge expense involved (the railroad would have insignificant commercial value), and even assuming that the involved international questions would be solved in favor of Russia, a port three hundred miles distant from Russia proper would not solve the problem.

The outlet from the Baltic to the ocean (4 on the map) is in Danish, Swedish, and German hands. Russia, which hopes to be the strongest power in the Baltic after Germany's defeat, will certainly look for privileges in the Kiel Canal. Most probably the canal will be put under international control, with the Scandinavian countries and Russia among the controlling states; Britain and, possibly, the United States, will also be among the membership.[10] But such an arrange-

10. In Teheran President Roosevelt proposed the erection of a tiny free state enclosing the Kiel Canal; the canal should be internationalized but left to the administration of the Kiel free state. "The Roosevelt improvisation fascinated Stalin. At its conclusion he arose, lumbered around the table and gravely shook hands with the President, saying, 'That is the solution; the right thing to do.' Churchill was reserved." Forrest Davis in *Saturday Evening Post*, May 13 and 20, 1944.

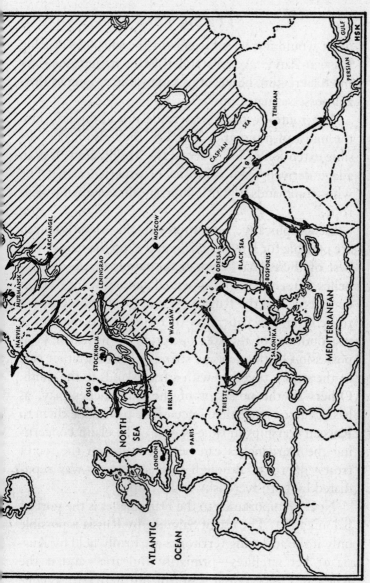

POSSIBLE POINTS OF SOVIET ACCESS TO THE SEA

ment would not be sufficient for the purposes of a big Russian Navy. A unilateral Russian dominance over the Kiel region, however, is impossible so long as Britain possesses naval power.

The routes to the Mediterranean lead directly into the midst of international affairs; they also make possible extension of influence in the Middle East. It is an adage derived from centuries of experience that "he who commands the Mediterranean commands Europe."

Geographically, four routes to the Mediterranean are possible for Russia (5, 6, 7 and 8, on the map). The best of these, that through the straits of the Dardanelles (7), is the main route used up to now by Russian commerce and the Russian Navy. It is the only direct route from Russian ports to the seas and oceans. A precondition of the free operation of a great navy is possession of the decisive strips of land on either side of the straits, together with a few islands to the south. Otherwise the possessor of the Dardanelles may, as has occurred more than once in the past, close them to Russian warships in time of war. The claim concerning the Dardanelles can be based also on the secret treaty of 1915, although this agreement was repudiated by both Kerensky and Lenin.

Next in importance to the Dardanelles is the port of Salonika (6). The use of Salonika by Russia is possible only if the adjoining territories are firmly held by Russia or her satellites—primarily Bulgaria—and if the whole of Greece, or at least, the northern part, is controlled by Russia. This outlet to the Aegean would bring Russia to the immediate vicinity of the British sphere. The wartime division of spheres between Russia and Britain practically gave Russia all the areas which lay on the way to Salonika—Rumania and Bulgaria—while Greece, with Salonika, remained in the British zone. The Greek EAM-ELAS movement, controlled by Communists, was prepared to return the Salonika region to the future Macedonian state which must constitute a component of a Balkan federation. In this way Salonika would pass from the British to the Russian sphere. Churchill's action against the ELAS uprising in December, 1944, was actually aimed against creation of this Soviet foothold in the Mediterranean.

Yugoslav ports (5) (or Trieste), lying much farther from Russia, are even less favorable than these others because of the expense involved and because they can be safely used only if the whole of the Balkans is firmly under Russian control. The way through Turkey to Syria (8) presupposes territorial annexations and new railroads from the southwestern Caucasus to the Mediterranean. This way also leads directly into the British sphere dominated by Cyprus.

The Trans-Iranian road (9) has no practical importance in relation to a naval base. It is a long and expensive road; its dominance would involve conquest of the whole of Iran; and it leads into the narrow Persian Gulf, entirely ruled by the British Navy.

Actually the most important routes, therefore, are those leading to the Eastern Mediterranean. If the

Soviet Government returns to its program of a big navy it will have to try to acquire one or several of these routes.

Russia can be safe without being a first-class sea power; but if she chooses to enter the naval competition and should aim to rise to front rank among the sea powers, she will have to look for the solution, in her favor, of controversial territorial problems of the highest complexity, in the sorest spots of world politics.

VI

BETWEEN GERMANY AND RUSSIA

THERE is no no man's land in any system of world policy. Power relations, like nature, abhor a vacuum. When a great state weakens and disintegrates it is as if dikes and dams were removed before the onrush of a mighty torrent. Streams burst from all sides into the political vacuum.

Recent generations have more than once witnessed this phenomenon in different parts of the world. Since the middle of the last century, China has been weakening, while other countries have grown much stronger. The consequences of this have been foreign intervention, partition, and dismemberment of China's territory, and incessant war. The whole political structure of Eastern Asia, shaken by the weakening of China, has become unstable, and is likely to remain so for a long time. Russia also, in 1917, disappeared temporarily from the ranks of the great powers. Within a matter of a few months, Japanese forces burst into Siberia, the Germans seized the Ukraine, France and Britain negotiated agreements concerning their spheres in Russia, and Poland started a military campaign to annex the Russian southwest. Turkey's role of "sick man" had become proverbial. From an immense empire she had shrunk to an almost insignificant nation. Her former territories were partly constituted as sovereign states of her various nationalities and partly acquired by the great powers—Britain, Italy, France, Russia, and Austria.

The disintegration in 1918 of the once powerful Austria-Hungary seemed at first to be an exception to the rule. A free Czechoslovakia, promising to develop into one of the most advanced of democracies, was arising out of the ruins of the century-old monarchy. A resurrected Poland was getting her lands back, and the world was happy to see a great historical injustice redressed. The southern Slavs, liberated from Austrian and Hungarian rule, were uniting within their own state. Austria and Hungary constituted themselves into two independent states of small size.

Neighboring these new nations in the east new small states were emerging from the disintegration of Imperial Russia, notably the Baltic States and Finland. A long line of new nations, most of them smaller in population than the State of New York, were created on the lands between the Arctic and the Adriatic, between Russia in the east and Germany in the west.

During the period between the two World Wars there existed in the zone between the Baltic and the Adriatic thirteen independent states with a total population, in 1939, of 126 millions, and comprising an area of 758,000 square miles. How important this part of Europe has been becomes obvious from the fact that its territory is more than four times as large as Germany's (182,000 square miles) and its population almost double that of Germany (69,600,000 in 1939).[1]

Not less than 40 per cent of the continent's population, exclusive of Russia, live in this zone. (If Russia is included, the percentage is 28). It is almost equal to the population of European Russia itself (140 millions in 1939).

From these figures it is clear how significant is this area which separates the two greatest nations of Europe. Its political coöperation with, or its opposition to, one of them might under certain circumstances be decisive for the course of history.

FRENCH PREDOMINANCE

AFTER the first World War it seemed that this new structure emerging on the site of the century-long

[1]. The Baltic-Adriatic zone, before the second World War, consisted of the following states (map p. 111):

	Area in sq. miles (*in thousands*)	1939 population (*in millions*)
1. Poland	150	35.1
2. Rumania	122	20.0
3. Yugoslavia	96	15.7
4. Czechoslovakia	54	15.2
5. Hungary	40	10.0
6. Greece	39	7.1
7. Austria	32	7.0
8. Bulgaria	34	6.3
9. Finland	127	3.8
10. Lithuania	20	2.0
11. Latvia	25	2.0
12. Estonia	18	1.1
13. Albania	11	1.1
	768	126.4

oppression of small nations by the big empires was a sensible, just, and democratic solution of the problem. As far as the international status of the new states was concerned, what danger could threaten them after Germany was decisively beaten? Nor did any danger appear to threaten the rest of Europe from the disintegration and division of Russia, one of the greatest and most powerful empires of the last centuries. The picture was a pleasant one.

But the rosy illusion did not last very long. Soon it began to be obvious that this region of Europe, so little known and so little understood by the world, was not only a multitude of nations but perhaps the most important element in the new structure of the old continent. It even became clear that the key to world war and peace problems was hidden under the soil of this Eastern zone of Europe.

After 1918 there was only one great power, France, on the continent of Europe. Never before had such a paradoxical situation existed—a situation resulting from the role which, for the first time in history, non-European powers had assumed in the solution of inner-European problems. Germany was beaten; Russia was extremely weak; Italy, whose military showing in the war had been poor, was a power of local significance only.

Because of this anomalous and tenuous state of affairs, the new and the old nations in this area saw no reason for the erection of a strong military federation. It seemed that France's good will and her army, combined with a loose connection among themselves, would suffice to safeguard their independence. This is why the emerging combinations of states were loose and unstable.

By 1919 the first threads were being woven to connect Czechoslovakia, Yugoslavia, Rumania, and Poland: these four nations were the biggest and the strongest of the small nations of the area, and their alliance would constitute the backbone of a strong federation. Soon after 1919 the first political agreements were signed. They connected, at the outset, pairs of nations: Czechoslovakia concluded a treaty with Yugoslavia (1920); Poland with Rumania (1921); Rumania with Czechoslovakia and Yugoslavia (1921). The treaty of alliance concluded in 1913 between Serbia and Greece was still in force. "There will arise a bloc," the Rumanian Foreign Minister, Take Jonesco, wrote in 1921, "of 85 million people controlling Central Europe from the Baltic to the Aegean Sea." [2]

The big bloc did not materialize, however. It soon became evident that divergent interests were splitting it into two parts, and that the absence of a real and immediate danger from without would allow to the members of the alliance much freedom and isolationism. Two nations bordering on Russia—Poland and Rumania—were united in an anti-Soviet policy which culminated in the Soviet-Polish War of 1920 and left a backwash of strong anti-Russian tendencies that in-

2. F. Jean-Destieux, *La paix n'est pas faite*, p. 15.

fluenced their policies of the '20's and '30's. Czechoslovakia, Yugoslavia, and Rumania formed the Little Entente, for protection against the German and Hungarian danger but not against the Russian. A Baltic group was formed by Poland, Latvia, and Estonia. A fourth group, finally, was created by the "Balkan Pact" of 1934 uniting Yugoslavia, Greece, Rumania, and Turkey.

Of these alliances the most interesting and the most important was the Little Entente. The gradual development of this combination of states was leading toward a superstate or a federative state, which, if it evolved further, would soon have created a most important state formation within Central Europe, embracing a population of 50 millions, certain industrial regions, and strong armies. A State Council of the Little Entente was created as a permanent agency, with a permanent secretariat, for the better coördination of foreign policies. A standing Economic Council was to serve to promote economic collaboration. Each in turn represented the group as a whole in the League of Nations. Finally, it was agreed that one of the aims of the federation would be coördination of their treaties with other states.

Other alliances between the nations of the region were not as closely knit as the Little Entente. The deeper aim of all of them was to overcome the provinciality, helplessness, and isolation of the small nations —the "Balkanization" of Central Europe.

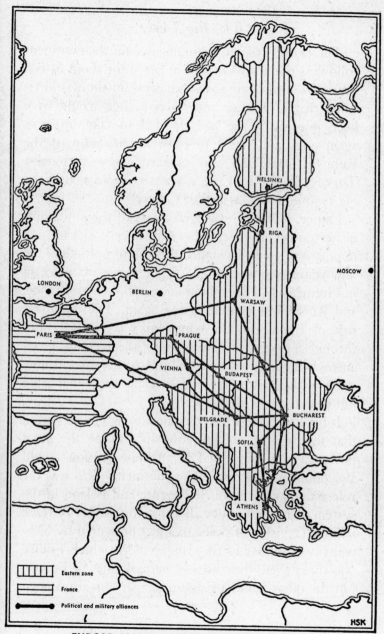

EUROPE 1919-34. FRENCH PREDOMINANCE

III

The era of French predominance on the continent following the first World War lasted for about fifteen years, from 1919 to 1934. No army in the world rivaled that of France and no resistance would have been possible if she had decided to take up arms again. Germany tried to resist her invasion of the Ruhr in 1923 and was crushed. New nationalist Turkey, backed by France, was victorious against the old regime as well as against Greece.

France, however, was well aware of the limitations of her power. Possessing only 9 per cent of Europe's population, she had assumed the task of upholding the new status quo and of taking the dominant place in it. Germany had 20 million more people than France, and Russia was certain to rise again. The dominant role of France on the continent was possible only through a system of firm military alliances and guarantees which would bind France to the old and new states of the Eastern region, especially those that arose out of defunct Austria-Hungary.

It became clear at the very beginning of this period that in the new configuration of Europe the great power which dominated the Middle Region would also dominate the rest of the continent. This was the role assigned to the Little Entente and Poland in the system of French policy. Because the danger to these nations (revision of peace treaties) presented by Germany was similar to the dangers with which France was threatened, they became natural allies of France. On the other hand, a Russian danger also threatened certain of these states. France's policy acquired an anti-Russian color, since her role was that of ally as well as protector.

All the Eastern alliances were backed by France. A treaty of alliance between France and Czechoslovakia was signed in January, 1924, a treaty of friendship with Rumania was concluded in June, 1926, and with Yugoslavia in November, 1927. The alliance with Poland was signed in February, 1921. In October, 1925, when France joined the other great powers in signing the Locarno treaties, she again signed treaties of "mutual guarantee" with Poland and Czechoslovakia in order not to weaken her Eastern support. Conventions of a military kind were also prepared. It was an axiom of French policy that aggression against one of her Eastern allies would mean a declaration of war by France against the aggressor.

This was the basis of continental power relations before 1935. Without her Eastern allies and protégés, France would be lost. French protection of the Middle Region was the very basis of the European structure and the stability of this structure lasted only as long as the Middle Region moved in the French orbit.

GERMAN PREDOMINANCE

BY THE middle of the '30's the happy quiescence of the status quo and of French hegemony was approaching its end. Three great powers bordering on the nations of the Middle Region were exhibiting increased

113

resentment toward the predominance of France—
Germany, Italy, and Russia. Of the three, Germany
was by far the strongest, and Hitler's success in 1933
signaled the emergence of a new aspirant for the role
of leader in Europe.

National Socialist Germany was fully aware of the
significance of the Middle Tier in the system of European power relations. Not only everyday practice but
the "science" of the "geopolitical school" pointed to
the East as the road to resurrection. The road from
Berlin to Paris leads through Warsaw, Prague, and
Bucharest: this geographical nonsense was not political nonsense. Germany learned it from the history
of the first World War, and, in general, from the
long experience of her *Ostpolitik*. She incorporated
this experience in the Brest-Litovsk Treaty with Russia. Hitler, himself a son of multinational Austria-
Hungary, was better aware of the significance of the
Middle Region than most leaders of other nations.
His political moves during the early years of his regime were evidence of a well-thought-out scheme of
gradual conquest of Europe which must begin in the
East.

Over a long period of time he emphasized again
and again that no claims to French territory, not even
to Alsace-Lorraine, were fostered by Germany; no
grounds existed, therefore, for conflicts in the West.
Hitler's activity was directed to the East. His "peaceful struggle" for the Eastern zone was persistent, sys-

tematic, and clever. He was aware that once he ruled these territories, the rest of Europe would be impotent against him.

In effect, the combination of Germany with the countries of the Eastern zone would create an empire with a population of about 200 million people, as compared with 140 millions in the West of continental Europe. The agrarian sections of the great empire (Rumania, Hungary, the Balkans) would make Germany's food situation secure in case of war; Germany's industry, the second in the world and the mightiest in Europe, would give the new empire a superiority over the war industries of its enemies. German manpower would be enormous. Germany would be invincible, at least in the Old World area.

Before the first year of the National Socialist regime in Germany had ended, the first blow was struck at France's Eastern bastion. In January, 1934, Poland signed a nonaggression treaty with Germany. The full significance of this agreement, the effect of whose announcement was attenuated by much diplomatic phraseology, was perceived by only a few persons. In reality this was the beginning of the end of France's era of control of the continent. In a sense it was a prelude to the second World War.

It was the astonishing lack of comprehension of the enormous importance of the Middle Region in world affairs that accounted for the generally optimistic reaction to the German-Polish pact. A pact means peace, some said. Poland's frontiers bordering Germany have become secure, others remarked. Is it not a sign that Hitler can be lived with?

"Any real improvement in German-Polish relations," wrote the London *Saturday Review* on February 2, 1934, "is to be accounted a positive gain for the peace of Europe. The eastern frontiers of Germany have long been the chief danger zone of the continent, and the menace to peace in that area must be considered as sensibly mitigated . . . The German-Polish pact appears to settle the matter for the next ten years."

Vernon Bartlett, a member of the House of Commons, expressed the typical reasoning. Nationalist Germans, he said, hate Poland and nourish hopes of a conquest of her territories; therefore Hitler's pact with Poland means a defeat for these Nazi Imperialists: "Many Germans will regret this repudiation of Herr Rosenberg's policy of expansion to the east," he said.

Following in Germany's steps, Italy was hammering at the gates of the Little Entente from the south. The "Rome Protocols" of March, 1934, following immediately after the German-Polish pact, were directed against Yugoslavia; they were an agreement between Italy and Austria and Hungary. Italy started arming the Yugoslav "Ustashi" (rebels) the same year. It was another Italian challenge to the Little Entente when Austria resolved in 1935 to reintroduce obligatory military service. The pressure grew.

Things became ominous when in March, 1937, Belgrade, without the consent of the other members of the young alliance, signed a five year nonaggression pact with Rome which corresponded to the German-Polish pact in the north.

There then followed the series of attacks, at short intervals, on France's Eastern fortress. In March, 1938, Germany annexed Austria. In September, 1938, she acquired the Czechoslovak Sudetenland. In October of the same year she raised the question of the Polish Corridor.

Hitler's and Mussolini's penetration into Eastern Europe consisted of a dozen or so political acts. Each step was accompanied by a reassuring explanation. The ability and also the need to analyze the process as a whole were lacking outside Germany and Italy. When Austria was annexed by Germany, people abroad were saying, "After all the Austrians are of German nationality." When the Sudeten question was resolved in favor of Germany, the prevailing opinion was similar. Thus, the structure of the Eastern zone was collapsing in many spots long before the second World War began.

In December, 1938, German Foreign Minister von Ribbentrop visited Paris for "friendly negotiation" purposes, and Eastern Europe stood high on his agenda. After the Munich victory, however, Germany did not need to concentrate on small details of the problem. Ribbentrop's demand was large but simple: France must declare her complete disinterestedness in the Eastern nations and their policies. The significance of the Middle Region to France and Germany and to Germany's struggle for hegemony could not have been made clearer than by these negotiations at Paris.

The outcome of the conference was not clear. Germany insisted repeatedly that M. Bonnet, the French Foreign Minister, had accepted the German demand and that therefore Germany was justified in conducting her campaigns in the East against Prague and Warsaw, which followed almost immediately after Ribbentrop's visit. France officially denied this version of the negotiations. Little as Mr. Ribbentrop merits confidence, it nevertheless appears that the reply of France was not a simple and direct "no." How great France's concession was—it was a defeat, too—will one day become known.

When Mr. Sumner Welles, on behalf of President Roosevelt, visited Berlin and Paris in 1940, Herr Goering told him "with the utmost emphasis that at the time Ribbentrop visited Paris, on December 6, 1938, . . . Georges Bonnet, then French Foreign Minister, had assured him in the name of the French government that, as the result of the agreements at Munich, France would renounce all further interest in Eastern Europe and had stated specifically that France would refrain from influencing Polish policy in the future. . . ."

"I consequently asked the Marshal," Mr. Welles relates, "to repeat his statement. Goering turned to Dr. Schmidt, who it appeared had been present at Paris at the interview between Bonnet and Ribbentrop

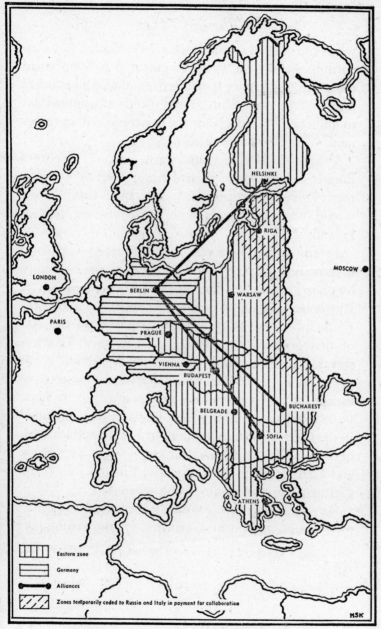

EUROPE IN THE GERMAN SCHEME 1938-42

119

Legend:

Eastern zone

Germany

Alliances

Zones temporarily ceded to Russia and Italy in payment for collaboration

Labels on map: LONDON, PARIS, BERLIN, PRAGUE, VIENNA, BUDAPEST, BELGRADE, ATHENS, SOFIA, BUCHAREST, WARSAW, RIGA, HELSINKI, MOSCOW

HSK

when the alleged commitments were made . . . According to him, the exact statement that Bonnet had made was that France thereafter renounced all political interests in Eastern Europe and specifically agreed not to influence Poland against the conclusion of an agreement with Germany . . ."

When Mr. Welles visited Paris, however, Georges Bonnet insisted that "he had never directly or indirectly given Germany any assurance that France would wash her hands with regard to the fate of Poland." [3]

In any event, between 1937 and 1941 Germany became real master of the East. Having paid off Italy by giving her the small territory of Albania, and Soviet Russia by agreeing to a Russian "sphere of interests" (September, 1939), Germany acquired all the rest of that great region. Austria was annexed; Czechoslovakia was occupied, divided, and practically annexed in 1939; Poland was defeated and annexed—except the Soviet part of it—in September of the same year. Hungary, Rumania, and Bulgaria were included in the German sphere by more or less peaceful means, between July, 1940, and January, 1941. Yugoslavia and Greece fell in 1941. Finally, Finland joined the German coalition in the spring of 1941.

At that period almost the whole of the Middle Region was controlled by Germany. Of the 126 million

3. Sumner Welles, *The Time for Decision* (1944), pp. 113, 114, 127.

inhabitants of the region, only a few million came under Italy's control; 22 million came under Russia. The rest of the population were put under the control of the Reich, which had a population of only 69 million.

Master of the entire region, Germany had actually won the European West before she began her war in Holland, Belgium, and France. In the framework of isolated Europe, Hitler's victory was a foregone conclusion from the moment he began to control the territories between the Baltic and the Adriatic Seas, because he who controls the Middle Region controls Europe. Before 1934 it was France, now it was Germany.

A profound difference became obvious, however, between the French and the German system of hegemony over the Eastern zone. In the internal affairs of the nations of that zone France was without power. Germany, on the contrary, interfered in every sphere of life. Under the French system the nations of the zone were coördinate elements; in the German system they were tools. The difference was due, first, to the general distinction between French democracy and German authoritarianism; secondly, to the weak will of French democracy in that interwar period; thirdly, and most important, to the geographical situation: France was in a position to exert influence by diplomatic and economic means only; her neighbor, Germany, stressed her *démarches* by the rumble of tanks and the rattling of sabers.

SOVIET PREDOMINANCE

WHEN the battle of Stalingrad was over, the Soviet Government started to elaborate its postwar programs. The plans were gradually growing and maturing; they were never presented in their entirety as an integral system. The Middle Region was the Number One item in these plans.

As far as Poland was concerned, the first impression gained of the Soviet demands (February-April, 1943) was that Soviet attention was focused mainly on the Curzon Line, while in reality dominance over the whole of Poland was the issue. In Yugoslavia, the government's War Minister, General Mikhailovich, was denounced by Moscow because of his "reactionary tendencies," while another government, which fitted in with the Soviet program, was being set up. The Czechoslovak Government unanimously consented to assume the role and the obligations of a member of the Soviet protectorate. Defeated Rumania overnight became an ally and turned over to Moscow the responsibility of direction of her international policy. Bulgaria followed.

As early as the summer of 1943 this part of the Soviet program was quite clear. The government was prepared, of course, to make certain concessions to its allies, for instance, to acknowledge British interests in Greece and the common interests of the allies in Austria. It did not leave any doubt, however, that the

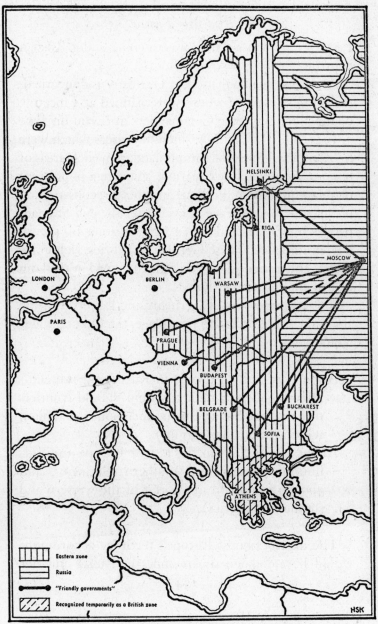

Eastern zone

Russia

"Friendly governments"

Recognized temporarily as a British zone

EUROPE IN THE SOVIET POSTWAR SCHEME

123

Eastern region as a whole was to come under Russian control.

As far as the occupation of Germany is concerned, the borders of the "zones" were defined at a meeting of the allied Supreme Commanders in Berlin on June 5, 1945. The Russian zone, including areas which were to be annexed by Russia and Poland, as well as areas of temporary military occupation, embrace a population of about 30 million. Political and social reconstruction of the zone would leave it, even after the end of occupation by Soviet military forces, a zone of special Soviet influence. These German territories, rich in industry and agriculture, would be the jewel in the long belt of the Eastern region.

If a reconstruction of Germany and Eastern Europe along these lines were to take place, the old continent would consist of:

About 275 million people in Russia and protectorates (about 135 million within the old frontiers of European Soviet Russia, and about 140 million within the smaller nations).

About 180 million in the rest of Europe (40 million in western and southern Germany, and about 140 million in the rest of the western and southern countries).

The distribution of Europe's territory accordingly would be 2,900,000 square miles in Russia and her sphere, and 1,000,000 square miles in the rest of Europe.

As far as the Soviet Union is concerned, the pattern of future developments is obvious. History has entrusted the leadership of Russia, during the war and postwar period, to a party and to a man whose concepts have for decades called for union with Germany —a transformed Germany, of course. From the end of 1918 until 1934, and perhaps until even more recently, the greatest hopes for the extension of Communism to the world have been pinned on Germany— the Number One nation in the long list of nations to be won over. An invincible bloc "from Aachen to Vladivostok" has been the favorite idea not only of Lenin but of the whole of his party. The war with Poland in 1920 was aimed not so much against Warsaw as toward direct contact with Germany. The internal crises in Germany during the period of the Weimar Republic were watched more closely in Moscow than anywhere else in the world. Hitler's rise to power was viewed in Moscow as an episode which would pave the way to the Communist transformation of Germany.

Stalin was the most ardent advocate of these concepts. He did not believe that any other possibilities for the spread of Communism existed. When the revolutionary movements in Germany subsided, after 1923, the Soviet leaders—Zinoviev, for instance— started a search for another "geography of the revolution" and pinned their hopes on China and India. Stalin remained cool and repudiated the new routes. The ebb of the revolutionary movement in Germany Stalin saw as a proof that the world had entered a temporary period of stability. The political crisis which began in the late '30's signified for Stalin the end of this "stability of capitalism" and the beginning of a new dynamic period, and the concept of a future Soviet-German collaboration was revived.

These concepts did not die during the war period. When they are revived, after the victory, they will mean: Rejection of any plan for a definite division of Germany into a multitude of small states; the setting up of a government, at least in a specified area of the former Reich, with a new pro-Soviet policy which will appeal to the rest of Germany to unite under it. When this program has been accomplished, a revival of German industry, in order to strengthen the great bloc, will become necessary.

TWO SPHERES IN EUROPE?

AT THE end of the first World War a British geographer, Halford Mackinder, wrote a short book entitled *Democratic Ideals and Reality*, a combination of geography and political science, or geography in its application to political problems. It was a profound study of outstanding European problems, rich in original thinking and of extreme interest even today— perhaps more interesting today than at any other time since its publication.

Mackinder was the father and founder of "geopolitics." German professors later vulgarized his theories and created a "geopolitical school" in favor of National Socialist political needs. From the abundance of Mackinder's ideas they took what fitted into the program of German conquest and finally settled on the vague, unscientific concept of *Lebensraum*. Mackinder himself had nothing to do with the German development of his ideas. On the contrary, the problem of making Europe secure from a possible new German aggression was one of his preoccupations.

"The condition of stability in the territorial rearrangement of East Europe is that the division should be into three and not into two state-systems. It is a vital necessity that there should be a tier of independent states between Germany and Russia. . . . Any mere trench-line . . . would have left German and Slav still in dual rivalry, and no lasting stability could have ensued."

The belt of nations between the Baltic and the Adriatic was designated by Mackinder the Middle Tier. The independence of the Middle Tier from its neighbors was accordingly a condition of a stable peace.

"Seven independent states, from the Adriatic to the Baltic, with a total of more than sixty million people, traversed by railways linking them securely with one another, and having access through the Adriatic, Black and Baltic Seas with the ocean, will together effectively balance the Germans from Prussia and Austria." [4]

If this condition is not fulfilled, and the Middle Tier falls to one of its big neighbors, this neighbor will be able "to rule Eastern Europe." (Eastern Europe, according to Mackinder's thesis, was the region between the Volga and the Elbe). Command of Eastern Europe, however, is in itself a source of great power, since it enables the ruler to achieve command of Northern Asia, too. Then the rest of Europe, of Asia and Africa must fall to the ruler of the "Heartland." (The "Heartland," in Mackinder's terminology, means the lands stretching from western Russia almost to the northern Pacific). He commands the "World-Island": Europe, plus Asia, plus Africa. And, finally, the rest of the world, too weak to resist, would fall to the ruler of the "World-Island."

"What if the Great Continent, the whole World-Island or a large part of it, were at some future time to become a single and united base of sea-power? Would not the other insular bases [Britain, America, Japan] be outbuilt as regards ships and outmanned as regards seamen? Their fleets would no doubt fight with all the heroism begotten in their histories, but the end would be fated."

Mackinder conceived his idea in these terms:

"Who rules East Europe commands the Heartland:

4. Halford Mackinder, *Democratic Ideals and Reality* (ed. 1942), pp. 158, 165.

"Who rules the Heartland commands the World-Island:

"Who rules the World-Island commands the World." [5]

More than twenty-five years—and what years!—have passed since these ideas were developed. Now the world is again, after the second World War, confronted with the same set of problems.

Most of the popular schemes proposed recently for postwar settlement of European relations envisage a durable partition of Europe into two rather than three spheres: the Eastern sphere, embracing all the large and small countries from a line east of Germany-Italy to the Urals; and the Western sphere, containing all nations lying west and south of Germany.

The British-Soviet twenty-year pact, concluded in 1942, was formulated on this basis: the two allies, considering themselves the leading powers of future Europe, reserved to themselves the solution of all outstanding European problems. The stated object of the pact, however, was "to render impossible the repetition of aggression and violation of peace by Germany." If the main postwar problem were to be the removal of the German menace, then the solution of the plaguing European problems must depend on the continuance of the war coalition of the two greatest powers of Europe. This was clear and logical. Al-

5. *Ibid.*, pp. 70, 150.

though the pact dealt with the future era of peace, it was purely a war product and to this extent was sensible and necessary. However, the war was not yet ended when the French-Soviet treaty of 1944 made the first puncture in the British-Soviet structure. It will not be the last.

In his *Time for Decision*, Mr. Sumner Welles likewise accepts the "regional system for Europe" in its Soviet version. "The Soviet government," he says, "is entitled to take such steps as it may judge best to create a regional system of Eastern Europe . . .

"The Soviet government is as legitimately entitled to promote a regional system of Eastern Europe, composed of co-operative and well-disposed independent governments among the countries adjacent to Russia, as the United States has been justified in promoting an inter-American system of the twenty-one sovereign American republics . . .

"To remove all grounds for justifiable criticism and to make doubly sure that the frontiers of future Russia will incorporate willing, rather than unwilling, Soviet citizens, the Soviet government would be well-advised to permit open plebiscites to be taken in every instance where there is a dispute as to the will of the majority . . ." [6]

But the twenty-one republics are really independent in their internal affairs, and their governments are not shaped in Washington. Elections, free from interference from outside, can therefore be held in South

6. Sumner Welles, *The Time for Decision*, pp. 332–334.

America. With Soviet Russia, on the other hand, there are but two alternatives: either a Soviet "regional system" with virtual incorporation of the smaller nations, without free plebiscite; or a free ballot and democracy —and no Soviet sphere. A combination of both is impossible. Therefore the Moscow government would encounter certain defeat if it followed Mr. Welles's advice.

This trend of thinking is not confined to a few authors and diplomats. On the contrary, the idea of dividing Europe into two spheres has a multitude of adherents because it seems to indicate a peaceful solution of thorny problems. The idea, an agreeable one, is being uncritically digested. However, it does not ensure a stable structure, nor does it contain a guarantee of peace.

The Soviet Government considers all nations bordering Russia in Europe a potential danger that must be dealt with by placing them under Soviet control. Actually, however, the nations of the Middle Region would only constitute a menace if they were to attempt to create one centralized and militarized state out of the various small nations; if they were to seek to revive Austria-Hungary, even if under new leadership. In that case Russia would be justified in opposing the emergence of a great new military power on her western borders, created artificially out of heterogeneous elements.

Contrary to the official view, a belt of independent

nations and regional alliances of these nations would present no menace for Russia, and it would be absurd to extend the Soviet state to the Adriatic, six hundred miles from Russia, in order to prevent little Yugoslavia from invading Russia; or to extend Russia's borders to Danzig, three hundred miles away, for the same reason. Soviet leaders are as well aware as others that control over the Middle Region is not a real way of insuring security. Were it not for other reasons, Moscow would not strive to widen its sphere of influence. However, these other reasons are not being stated frankly.

Nothing would serve better as a guarantee of Russia's real security than a really friendly attitude toward neighboring nations. And there is no other way to demonstrate friendliness toward a small neighbor than by leaving her the liberty to arrange her affairs as she pleases. Such a policy, especially in combination with a strong Russian Army, is by far the best guarantee against war and encroachment.

VII

THE POWERS IN THE MIDDLE EAST

THE Middle East has not been in the political limelight during the war; it has only sporadically attracted public attention. Nevertheless it is one of the chief sore spots in world affairs and its importance is bound to increase in the near future. The interests of the great powers clash here with a force comparable only to the clash of their antagonisms in the Far East or in Central Europe.

This part of the Asiatic continent, the Biblical cradle of humanity, which once embraced great civilizations, huge empires, and an ancient culture, is today one of the most backward countries in the world. Gone are the times of the califs, of the Thieves of Bagdad, the Thousand and One Nights, and the Tower of Babylon. Vast deserts—salt deserts, sand deserts, the Syrian, Keviz, and Lut deserts—cover the region, and lions and jackals are a danger to man. Poverty-stricken peoples populate the lands, half of them nomads on the lowest level of human culture. Disease and epidemics rage to an extent unknown elsewhere. Although enormous mineral riches are hidden beneath the earth of these nations, the backwardness and poverty of the peoples and political conditions have left this wealth untapped.

In the political sense these lands are situated between

Russia and the British sphere. The long narrow belt of land dividing Britain and Russia in the Middle East begins at the Dardanelles and ends deep in Central Asia at a point where Russia, Afghanistan, and Tibet meet. The belt is comprised mainly of three Asiatic nations —Turkey, Iran, and Afghanistan (see map, p. 135) with a combined population of about 40 millions. In a more general sense—racial, religious, cultural, and economic—other remnants of old Turkey also belong to this sphere: Arabia, Iraq, Palestine, and Syria, as well as some minor states of the Arabian peninsula. These territories, most of which have been since 1920 under British protectorate (Syria was under France), form a distinct part of the Middle East, and their fate, too, depends on the interrelationships between the Big Three. All together, these nations, with a total population of about 55 millions [1] constitute an important part of the Asiatic world. Their total area is greater

1.	Area (000 km.)	1939 population (000)
Afghanistan	650	7,000
Arabia (including Oman, Kuweit, Yemen, Hadhramaut)	2,600	7,000
Bahrein Isles	0.6	120
Iraq	302	3,700
Iran	1,644	15,000
Turkey	744	16,300
Palestine	26	1,502
Trans-Jordania	90	300
Syria and Lebanon	197	3,700
	6,253.6	54,622

The population figures are approximate. *League of Nations Yearbook,* 1941–42.

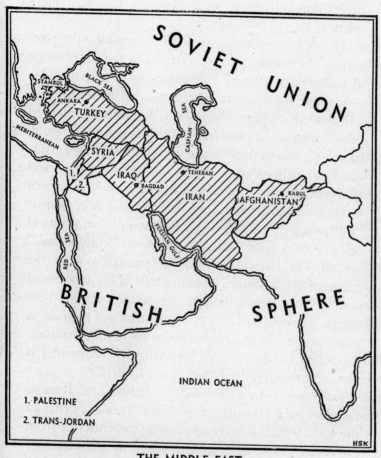

1. PALESTINE
2. TRANS-JORDAN

HSK

THE MIDDLE EAST

than the whole of Europe, excluding Russia; their population, however, is 20 per cent less than Germany's.

The Asiatic characteristics of this region—the poverty of the people, the deserts, the almost total absence of industry in general and war industry in particular—account for the main difference between this area and those European regions which, although situated between great empires, are able to resist, to struggle, to invent, and to impress the world. Here, in the Middle East, nations are independent only because, and to the extent that, the rivalry of the great leaves them to their independence. This is the classical region of "buffer states," of "spheres of influence," of political bribery on a large scale, of industrial "concessions," and of "oil diplomacy." Abdurrachman, one of the rulers of Afghanistan, has summarized his experience and wisdom concerning the great powers in these simple words: "Every government strives to seize as much as it can in the largest quantity." And therefore, according to him, "the White Dog [the Russians] is no better than the Red Dog [the British]."

For more than a century the British and Russian Empires have been drawing nearer to one another in the Middle East. Like two opposing torrents, one from the north, the other from the south, they have rolled to meet. Hating, fearing one another, they craved to approach at the same time.

Britain expanded outward from India in a fan-shaped movement, taking all the lands from Baluchistan to Burma. Russia moved through the Caucasus, around the Caspian, across Turkestan. Rolling forward, subduing on the way old kingdoms and alien races, they arrived, one from each side, at the frontiers of Tibet and Afghanistan in the last decades of the nineteenth century.

Since 1815 resistance to further Russian expansion in Europe has been strong. The dynamism of the empire therefore sought an outlet in Asia—in Central Asia as well as in the Far East. Chancellor Gorchakov, the well-known Russian diplomat of the '60's and '70's, was the first to state that "Russia's future lies in Asia," since she "has no great tasks to fulfill in Europe."

At the end of the Napoleonic era Britain's possessions were limited to territories in southern, central, and eastern India, while Russia's frontiers in Asia lay northeast of the Aral and Caspian Seas. Then, in 1818, Britain acquired the vast Rajputana territory and, moving north, in 1845 took Punjab in Kashmir. Russia came down and, in the 1840's, took Turgai and Akmolinsk. Between 1876 and 1883 Britain proceeded to annex Baluchistan, Russia annexed Turkestan during the '60's and '70's, and Merv in the '80's. Then, in 1895, Britain occupied the frontier provinces. Only the narrow tongue of eastern Afghanistan now lay between the expanding colossi.

It was obvious that if the course of expansion continued the two powers would one day find themselves with a common frontier in the Middle East. In 1810 the shortest distance between the Russian and the

British possessions in Asia was 1,100 miles; in the 1850's the distance was 500 miles; in the '80's it was only 300 miles—in the Pamirs, in Afghanistan, only 20 or 30 miles. A clash between Britain and Russia over Asiatic problems would have to be fought out elsewhere, too. Such a clash would develop into one of the greatest wars of Europe and Asia. To remove the danger and postpone the conflict, special agreements, typical of this part of the world, were from time to time concluded between London and St. Petersburg. It was agreed, for instance, not to build any railways in a neutral zone (Persia), not to establish consulates or send agents (Russia in Afghanistan), not to annex certain specific territories (Khiva). Most of these agreements, however, were shortlived. At the beginning of the twentieth century the crisis appeared to be approaching fast.

Britain and Russia were the masters of the Middle East in the nineteenth century; they still play this role today. Other powers have striven to acquire influence, economic privileges, and territory, but have not been successful to any important degree. During the time of the late Kaiser Germany penetrated through Turkey into Persia and even acquired some influence in Afghanistan; her Berlin-Bagdad railroad, planned to connect the German capital with the great Arabic world had done much to irritate British-German relations in the last years preceding the first World War, as did also the public utterances of the Kaiser, which pointed to Britain as the great enemy of the Islamic world. Again in the '30's Hitler's Germany acquired influence in the Middle East by political as well as economic means. This influence was eliminated in 1941–42.

The French colonial Empire had recoiled before Britain in this part of the world. At the end of the first World War France obtained only a mandate over Syria and Lebanon, with a population of about 3 millions. Certain oil rights were conceded to her by Britain in Iraq. But on the whole France's influence in the Middle East was not great. Italy, too, claimed territory in Asia Minor, when Turkish spoils were divided, but had to abandon her claims after the resurrection of the new Turkey early in the '20's.

During the war years, 1941 to 1945, Soviet activity in the Middle East in general was growing. Egypt was the first of the Arab countries to recognize the Soviet Union, and in August, 1943, a Soviet diplomatic agency was set up in Cairo. In the summer of 1944 diplomatic relations were established with Syria and Lebanon, former French mandates. The setting up of a consulate in Palestine was likewise contemplated. In September, 1944, relations between Iraq and the Soviet Union were established. Saudi Arabia conducted her relations with Moscow through Cairo, where the Soviet envoy and his staff were becoming an important center of Soviet political activity in a vast region.

The Arabs are an important element among the nations of the Middle East. So far as international relations are concerned, their importance lies in the fact that the Arabs, subjugated, frequently exploited, and extremely poor, for centuries have been a rebellious or a potentially rebellious element in a vast line of states and colonies. Numbering approximately 40 millions, they are dispersed over the Middle East and North Africa; from Iraq, Arabia, and Palestine their habitations extend into Tunis and Algeria. These lands comprise British and French possessions, spheres, mandates, wherein Arab and pan-Arab movements, at times patronized by Paris and London, have at other times been the cause of serious concern. A certain amount of anti-British feeling has existed in Arab lands for a long time. To a degree it is present even in the Arab League, recently established by the governments of the Arab nations. Soviet influence, having grown during the war, also made itself felt in the Arab world, especially in Syria, Palestine, and Egypt.

In Syria an important Armenian minority constitutes a link with the Soviet Armenian Republic. In the fall of 1944 a visit by Professor Abrahamian, dean of the Soviet Armenian University, to the Syrian Armenians was built up to a political event. On the other hand, it was expected that one of the Asiatic Soviet republics, with a Moslem majority, would soon establish direct diplomatic relations with Moslem Syria.

The part of another link to the Middle East was assigned to the small Kurd nationality, the members of which are dispersed over Iran, Turkey, and the Soviet Caucasus. In 1944 Soviet authorities tentatively began to promote a Kurd movement, in order to attract the sympathies of Kurds across the borders.

In other cases it was not the nationalist feelings of the nations of the Middle East but their religious orientation that furnished the key for the cautious Soviet penetration. The newly established Soviet religious authorities were claiming, through the Soviet Foreign Office, the property and the position which the Imperial Orthodox societies had acquired in Palestine and elsewhere. The new Soviet envoy, Abdul Sultanov, prayed every Friday in the mosque of Omar in order to strengthen contacts with the Moslems of Palestine. Simultaneously, the British-Zionist conflict has found its counterpart in a rapprochement between Moscow and Zionist groups.

For a long time Zionism was considered by the Soviet Government an anti-Soviet and pro-British movement; along with the persecution of Zionists in Russia the government forbade the teaching of the Hebrew language in Soviet schools. As far as Palestine and, in general, the Middle East are concerned, the Soviet Government supported Arab, rather than Jewish, nationalism. Since 1942–43 a general reversal has occurred in Soviet policy with regard to Palestine, Zionism, and the Jewish question. In 1943 the Soviet Vice-Commissar of Foreign Affairs, Ivan Maiski, visited Palestine, received delegations of Palestinian Jews and made reassuring declarations. A "leading Soviet diplomat" said to a similar Jewish delegation in 1943:

"Back in the 'twenties we could not but consider

Zionism as an agency of British imperialism. And we were bound to treat you accordingly. Now, however, the whole situation has changed. Not only Britain and Zionism seem to be at a constant variance, but our outlook, too, has undergone a serious evolution. Should Soviet Russia be interested in the future in the Middle East, it would be obvious that the advanced and progressive Jews of Palestine hold out much more promise for us than the backward Arabs controlled by feudal cliques of Kings and effendis." [2]

In November, 1943, the Palestinian question was raised by Stalin at the Teheran Conference. Two delegates of a Moscow Jewish Committee visited America early in 1944 and spoke in public meetings about a world-wide "brotherhood of Jewry." These Soviet moves were motivated by opposition to Britain's predominance in the Middle East.

At least 90 per cent of the population of the Middle East are Moslems, and religion plays a far greater role in these regions than elsewhere in the world. Politically this fact is of enormous importance, for a common religion binds the Moslems of this region to 75 million Moslems in British India and between 20 and 25 million Moslems in Russia. The Mohammedans of the buffer states, therefore, can serve as a bridge of influence leading from the Russian to the British possessions, or vice versa. Soviet Russia has often made

2. Eliahu Ben-Horin, "The Soviet Wooing of Palestine," *Harper's Magazine*, April, 1944.

use of this bridge at important moments during her conflicts with London.

Of the eleven Soviet republics which constituted the Soviet Union in 1939, eight are situated on the borders of this Asiatic Middle Tier.[3] In most of them the Moslem population is in the majority and serves as a center of appeal to the Moslems of the neighboring lands under British rule. One of the aims of the Soviet constitutional reform of February, 1944,[4] was to contrast the condition of these Moslems with the treatment accorded Moslems in India and the mandated territories.

The most important developments, however, took place in Iran and Turkey. These are discussed in subsequent chapters.

The United States was the last among the great powers to acquire interests in the Middle East. The history of its activities in this area has been different from that of the other great powers: it began with private economic investments involving no territorial acquisitions or questions of influence. Nevertheless, political influence grew rapidly and, within a period of twenty years, has assumed a peculiar role athwart the two dominating powers.

3. Georgia, Armenia, Azerbaijan, Turkomen, Uzbek, Tadzhik Kazakh, Kirghiz.
4. The reform granted the Union republics the right to independent foreign relations and maintenance of independent armies. These rights, of no consequence practically, were designed, in the Middle East, to facilitate political ties with the buffer states and the British zone.

The Big Three

IN THE past, one of the chief means of political penetration into these regions has been the construction of railroads. In a loosely united state, like the states of the Middle East, a new railroad opens up the region and acts as an economic as well as a political magnet. Foreign capital needed for its construction is invested only with the advance consent of the foreign government. The reliable police force required to operate a railroad must sometimes be imported along with the locomotives and the engineers. The railroads of the backward lands—the Berlin-to-Bagdad, the Manchurian, and the African railroads, for instance—were considered political strongholds of the parent nations.

The importance of the railroads as a means of political penetration has been overshadowed during the last three or four decades by another means—the development of oil resources. The Middle East is one of the richest oil territories of the world. From Russian Baku on the Caspian down through Iran, Iraq, and Arabia the territory is a great oil region. Its reserves have never been thoroughly explored; experts differ in their estimates. Recent American explorations estimate the subterranean oil riches of the Middle East, exclusive of those of Russia, at 50 billion barrels.

It is because of its oil riches that the Middle East has attracted so much interest in the last decades. Were it not for the oil, whose importance has been increasing rapidly in the eyes of every power in the world, this region would certainly not be so important today in world politics. Since the invention of the automobile and later the airplane, the war industry of every nation has been dependent on oil; nations which do not possess important oil reserves beneath their own surface—such as Britain, France, Germany, Japan—have been endeavoring to secure for themselves supplies from other parts of the globe, and the Middle East has been paramount among the objects of their oil policies.

"The Middle East," Secretary of the Navy Frank Knox said, "contains the greatest known pool of oil in existence in the world. The ordinary man cannot imagine the wealth of this region. The oil here could create a hundred Rockefellers." [5] "The center of gravity of world oil petroleum is shifting from the Gulf of Mexico–Caribbean area [and from the United States] to the Persian Gulf area," was the opinion of the geologist Everett Lee DeGolyer, after his investigation of the oil regions of the Middle East for the American Government late in 1943. He arrived at the conclusion that the "indicated" reserves of Iran amount to 3 to 4 billion barrels; of Saudi Arabia, 2 to 7 billions; of Kuweit, 9 billions; and of the whole Middle Eastern region, 50 billion barrels. How large these quantities are is obvious from the fact that the total world output amounts to 2 billion barrels a year.

The development of the oil resources of the Middle East, which began only about forty years ago, has

5. *Fortune*, June, 1944.

developed at such a pace that this region, of secondary importance in modern history, is in process of becoming one of the most important battlegrounds in the economic wars of the powers.

Almost every world power is represented in the Middle East, and the economic battle fronts here correspond to the grouping of the powers elsewhere. It was natural that Britain should have been first to make her appearance there; that Germany should swoop down following the British traces; that France should make a vigorous demand for some of the oil as her share for bringing about the victories of World War I; that the United States should have been the last to land in a region under foreign control; and that Russia should stand aside and, watching every move of the powers, be ready to counteract these moves if and when they approached a potential Russian sphere in the Middle East. The relationships of the powers in the Middle East were exact duplicates of their combinations, groupings, conflicts, and alliances in the larger *Weltpolitik*.

Actual business competition between oil companies in the Middle East was limited. Rather agreements between them divided the great region into zones and markets—into separate spheres of the companies. After the first World War London and Paris tried to exclude America from the oil business of the region, and a prolonged diplomatic conflict arose between the Foreign Office and the State Department. While Lord Curzon and Bainbridge Colby were exchanging lengthy notes and discussing the legal aspects of the term "mandated territories," the oil companies of the two countries found a common ground, talking in terms of barrels, markets, pounds sterling, and dollars. They soon reached an agreement which subsequently developed into a unified system of joint activity in the Middle East. The so-called Red Line Agreement between British and American oil companies prohibited these companies from proceeding individually. This agreement, which is still in force, embraced the whole Middle East except Iran.[6] Agreements, however, did not do away entirely with rivalry and antagonisms. They have continued to exist until today, at times bursting into the open. In general, however, economic collaboration between America and Britain has nowhere made greater progress than in the Middle East during the last ten or fifteen years. It may serve as a classic example of internationalization of economic activities.

The British companies, the oldest customers of the Middle East, enjoyed the strong backing of their government; the American companies, on the other hand, were more energetic, more enterprising, and better equipped financially. American economic expansion in the Middle East was progressing in 1942–45, at first without any direct interference of the American Government. However, it soon became obvious that a certain amount of government backing was necessary. In June, 1943, when the Petroleum Reserves Corpora-

6. *Foreign Policy Report,* July 1, 1944, Blair Bolles.

tion was created by the government, with Secretary of the Interior Harold Ickes at its head, one of its objectives was an increase in the American oil output in Asia and one of its first projects, in competition with Britain, was to build a great pipe line from Arabia to the Mediterranean in order to facilitate and augment the shipments of oil and to reduce their costs.

In December, 1943, Mr. Ickes stated, in an article in the *American Magazine*, that the oil reserves of the United States are not sufficient for more than fourteen years; that the war is being conducted throughout the world chiefly with American oil; and that in order to conserve American resources the United States must expand the production of oil in other lands. In accordance with this view of the government, the Petroleum Reserves Corporation reached an agreement with the Arabian-American Company: the government was prepared to invest about $150,000,000 for construction of the pipe line.

Mr. Ickes' estimate of the oil reserves of the United States was generally disputed and opposition was expressed to the project of a direct state enterprise. From London, which had not been consulted, came other ideas and projects. Eventually, the pipe-line plan was dropped, and there were even doubts as to whether the plan had ever been seriously considered. What remained from the passionate discussions of those months has been the growing interest of the United States Government in oil enterprises abroad. It was not only oil companies that conducted negotiations and concluded agreements: now Mr. Cordell Hull, the Secretary of State, was taking part in conferences with Lord Beaverbrook, the delegate of the British Government. Government activity was far more important now than even in the early '20's, when the British were for the first time compelled to move over a bit in the Middle East and to concede a share to the Americans.

On August 8, 1944, an Anglo-American oil agreement was signed in Washington. Acknowledging the interests of "other producing and consuming countries" (Russia among them), the agreement, for the time being, however, foresaw the creation of a purely Anglo-American "International Petroleum Council," consisting of eight members: four American and four British. A short time later the United States Government withdrew the agreement from the Senate for revision. A new draft, completed in February, 1945, was the subject of renewed discussion with London. Conclusion of an agreement was considered certain. As far as the future Anglo-American Petroleum Council is concerned, the new draft of agreement made no changes.

In 1944–45 the oil markets of the world were more firmly held by America and Britain than at any time previously. With their interests interwoven, they were approaching a united front and an almost total monopoly of the world's oil trade. Meantime, France and Holland, also interested in oil, were being weakened by the war.

The results of the Anglo-American collaboration

in the three main oil-concession countries of the Middle East are the following:

Saudi Arabia is the exclusive American oil sphere. The Arabian-American Oil Company (owned by Standard Oil of California and the Texas Company) is in possession of two large oil concessions in Saudi Arabia; the concession runs until the year 2000. The company began its shipments in 1939, and only limited use has so far been made of the contracted rights. A large increase is probable. The concession in Saudi Arabia is of particular interest from a political point of view, since that country is actually a British sphere wherein the American oil business has made use of the open door principle in the widest sense, even to the extent of practically excluding British competition. Saudi Arabia's oil production amounts to only 11 per cent of the total Middle Eastern output, but has prospects of rapid growth.

Iraq, producer of 20 per cent of the oil of the Middle East, is an example of the reverse kind. The only important oil company is the Iraq Petroleum Company, which consists of British, American, and French interests. America possesses 23.75 per cent of the shares and the same percentage of oil produced in Iraq.

Iran, with her 65 per cent output, is the oldest of the established Middle Eastern oil fields. Britain has a hold on Iranian oil through the Anglo-Iranian Oil Company and subsidiaries. For more than thirty years the British Government has been in possession of at least 50 per cent of the company's capital. It was Win-

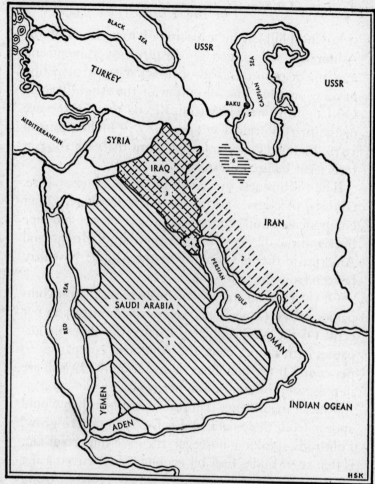

1. Saudi Arabia. USA

2. Iran. Mostly British

3. Iraq. British and USA, 22½% each

4. Kuwait. British and USA, 50% each

5. Baku. Center of Russian oil

6. Unexplored oil lands in Iran

OIL INTERESTS IN THE MIDDLE EAST

ston Churchill, in his capacity of First Lord of the Admiralty, who urged the British Government and Parliament onto the road of direct state participation in oil economy. The oil output of the Anglo-Iranian Oil Company has risen from 81,000 tons on the eve of the first World War (1913) to 10 million tons in 1938. Its huge concession runs until the year 1993; it feels itself secure in Iran.

The oil business in the Middle East, as elsewhere, consists, of course, not of the oil wells alone. Other components of oil economy are the refineries and pipe lines and the oil fleet. The relationship of Britain and America in the oil economy of the Middle East may be seen from the following figures:

Of the total oil reserves of this region, British companies possess 60 per cent, American companies 33 per cent. Of the total refinery capacity the British companies own 80 per cent, the American companies 20 per cent. Of the pipe lines in operation the British are in possession of almost 100 per cent.[7]

American influence is in reality stronger than would appear from these data, and it is continuing to grow. Politically speaking, however, the most important fact is that the Middle East oil economy has woven a net of British-American interests which receive strong support from the British and, to a lesser but growing degree, from the American Governments. "In the Middle East," a report of the Foreign Policy Association said, "It is difficult to distinguish rivalry between

7. *Fortune*, June, 1944.

companies from rivalry between states." Likewise, agreements and collaboration between the oil companies always correspond to the national policies of their respective governments. The recent oil agreements between America and Britain mean "a first step in what might be a carefully laid plan of a superstate cartel" [8] with all its far-reaching political implications. A superstate cartel is primarily a cartel of Britain and America, which today control 80 per cent of the world's oil.

For the grouping of powers in the Middle East, the new position of the United States is the most important event. It was significant that after the Cairo conference in February, 1945, two of the conferees, Mr. Roosevelt and Mr. Churchill, met the heads of state of Saudi Arabia, Egypt, and Ethiopia to discuss current political problems of the Middle East. Likewise significant was the statement made by the King of Iran, at about the same time, concerning America: "Iran welcomes signs that a positive and crystallized United States foreign policy is developing for the first time in the Middle East; after the war and the evacuation of foreign troops from Iranian soil this country looks forward to increasing economic ties with America." [9]

Senator Burton correctly summarized the prevalent trend when he stated, in his report on his overseas trip,

8. In the words of Mr. J. K. Pew of the Sun Oil Company. *Fortune*, October, 1944.
9. *New York Times*, March 8, 1945.

that "the Middle East and North Africa are a proving ground for a constructive vigorous foreign policy of the United States." [10]

REVOLUTIONS AND NATIONALISM

SINCE 1918 Moscow has been appealing to the peoples of all Asia, from Turkey to China, to rise against the imperialist powers, and has been promising help and coöperation. In the Soviet view a social revolution, in its Asiatic aspect, did not call for immediate socialization and drastic economic upheavals on the Russian pattern but rather for an uprising against imperialism and, first of all, against Britain. It called for overthrow of the internal political system, creation of new governments, rejuvenation of the state machinery, creation of strong military forces, certain agrarian changes, a holy war against the "conquerors and enslavers," resurrection of the nationhood and rehabilitation of backward peoples—Arabs, Turks, Hindus, Afghans, Chinese, Persians—for a common opposition to the "international robbers," and close alliance with Soviet Russia. It was a vision of a general uprising of the Asiatic peoples with Moscow at the helm.

The anti-British spirit of the Soviet policy was its strongest element during the whole interwar period. To Moscow it appeared obvious that a war with Britain in the very near future was inevitable and that such a war would have to be fought in the Middle East.

10. *New York Times*, February 23, 1945.

"That the main instigator of a war against us will be England cannot be doubted," wrote A. Sultanzade, one of the chief expounders of Soviet Middle Eastern policies. "He who has not understood this truth has not understood anything in the world. The chief battleground will be the Middle and the Near East. In all English plans Iran is being considered as the main base for deploying armed forces." [11]

This Soviet policy produced in the Middle East reactions of hatred toward England which at times were even stronger than the violent propaganda of Moscow itself, and this hatred was the driving force behind a big revolutionary movement. "Liberation" in the Middle East meant not only an internal upheaval, as in Europe, but first of all liberation from foreign control, which was British control in ninety-five out of a hundred cases. Whereas in Europe revolutions were often antinationalist, in the Middle East nationalism was the strongest element of the revolutionary movement.

After World War I revolutionary movements spread all over Asia; new nationalist leaders emerged overnight; old customs, habits, kings, and lords were overthrown. In every land a new great national hero was rising to lead the people. Having attained success in a bloody struggle with his predecessors, he remained as leader of his "regenerated nation"; having defied the influence of Britain and France, he was becoming the

11. A. Sultanzade, *The Economic Development of Persia* (Moscow, 1930), p. 11.

standard bearer of peoples "awakened to freedom and independence." [12]

In Turkey after a century of Turkish degeneration it was Mustapha Kemal Pasha who defied the Sèvres Treaty, overthrew the old regime, and achieved a unique position. In Persia, Reza Khan had a similar career. In Afghanistan, Ammanullah was the great reformer of the '20's. In China, Chiang Kai-shek, succeeding Sun Yat-sen, was the revolutionary hero. Friendship with Moscow was their first political commandment, and all of them were warmly greeted by Moscow. It was indeed a great movement on the part of the Asiatic peoples.

12. Here, for instance, are eloquent excerpts from an article written by a prominent Turkish nationalist in the early '20's; it was typical of the political atmosphere of the East:

"One thing stands out definite, unshakable, eruptive like a volcano, stable and firm like one's faith in God, infinite like time and darkness: HATRED AGAINST THE BRITISH.

"In their vocabulary impudence stands for sangfroid; meanness and vileness for truthfulness; insolence, hatred and despotism for virtue and civilization . . .

"If the columns on which religion stands are four, there should be a fifth one: HATRED AGAINST THE BRITISH.

"A Christian who is proud of his divine and Jewish ancestry, and who is anxious to get nearer to Jesus and Holy Mary should rest on one sole conviction: HATRED AGAINST THE BRITISH."

The article concluded:

"Therefore, for God's sake, Massacre! For the love of your country, Massacre! In the name of crying humanity, Massacre! In revenge for your dead brethren, Massacre! For the salvation of the world and the peace of hell, Massacre! . . . On the day of your victory all the world will spit on the shameless face of the British . . ." Bierstadt, *The Great Betrayal* (New York, 1924), p. 80.

Then in the middle and at the end of the '20's came the reversal. Sons of nationalist revolutions, the new leaders one after another began to revise their international policies. There was no prospect of success in endlessly combating the imperialism of the great powers; there was certain danger in a one-sided alliance with Russia; there was a growing fear of possible territorial and other demands on the part of Moscow. Often, the activity of local Communist parties was creating animosity against Russia and accelerating the reversal.

Opposing Britain, fearing Russia, the new leaders sometimes looked for a third power as an ally: Germany? America? It was, in Nietzsche's phrase, a case of love for the remote rather than love for the neighbor. Such was the case in Iran, to a certain degree in Iraq, and among the Arabs in Palestine. Others of the nations reverted to collaboration with Britain and, in the Far East, with America. Russia was once more gradually being isolated and relations between her and her Asiatic neighbors during the '30's were cooling off.

TURKEY AND THE POWERS

"TURKEY must be finished up"—such was the last Tsar's marginal note to a report of August, 1916, concerning Russian war aims. Indeed, had the Russian Revolution not occurred, the Turkish state might have ceased to exist a quarter of a century ago.

For a hundred and fifty years the expanding empire of the north was pressing the great empire of the south.

Turkey was becoming Russia's "hereditary enemy." What are today the southern Ukraine, Crimea, Bessarabia, the Caucasus, once belonged to Turkey. Russian victories helped the Balkan Slavs, as well as Rumania, in their struggle against Turkey for independence. During the nineteenth century Turkey was reduced to the size of a second-rate power, comprising, however, a not unimportant part of the Middle East. Her population on the eve of the first World War was approximately 28 millions.

It was fatal for Turkey that her main possessions lay across and around the British life line to India. A strong Turkey, able to collaborate with Britain's enemies—France, and, later, Germany—would be a menace to the British Empire. Britain therefore offered only sporadic aid to the Turks, primarily, in their opposition to Russia. Squeezed between Russia and Britain, losing one war after another, siding in coalition wars with the wrong party, Turkey, as if guided by an unlucky star, disintegrated. At the end of the first World War she was close to annihilation.

Secret agreements (1915–17) between Britain, France, and Russia (later Italy) anticipated an almost complete partition of Turkey among the Allies. The largest acquisitions were destined to go to Britain and Russia, while Italy and France were to be content to take smaller territories in Asia Minor. Britain's anticipated acquisitions embraced the oil lands of Iraq and Arabia as well as Palestine. In the final arrangements France obtained even less than was planned for her,

Italy almost nothing, and Britain was the only party for whom the program materialized.

Russia's acquisitions of territory in Turkey, as agreed upon by the Allies, were to be twofold. In Europe she was to obtain the Dardanelles, the Sea of Marmara, and the adjoining territories. Possession of Constantinople and the Dardanelles had been a prime goal of Russian policy for more than a century. Now for the first time London gave her agreement, notwithstanding a thousand doubts concerning the emergence of a naval rival in the Eastern Mediterranean. Winston Churchill, a member of the then British Government, was preparing in 1915 a great naval action against Turkey; the alliance with Russia demanded political collaboration and sacrifices. However, the attack was not successful, and Constantinople remained unoccupied during the war.

The territories in Asia to be ceded to Russia under the agreements were even more extensive. A large section of Turkish territory bordering on the Caucasus (see map, p. 172) was slated for future Russian acquisition. As early as 1878 Turkey, following a military defeat, ceded a part of these lands to Russia, and it was only in the face of a British-French war threat against Russia that St. Petersburg (at the Berlin Congress) renounced the clauses of the peace treaty applying to a part of these territories. Never abandoning its goal in this direction, however, the Russian Government watched Turkish policy closely in Turkish Armenia, where the notorious Armenian massacres repeatedly perpetrated by the Turks furnished occasion for foreign intervention.

In 1912 the Russian Government forced Turkey to begin negotiations leading to international control over these territories; in 1914 Turkey declared her agreement.[13] Had war not broken out, the lands of Turkish Armenia and probably also the adjoining regions would have become Russian. The Russian demands were among the reasons which led Turkey to join Germany in the war. What Russia had expected to gain before 1914 now became part of her war program.

Annexations of territories in Asia Minor adjoining the Caucasian borders were planned on a different scale. By the terms of a secret agreement with her allies (August, 1916) Russia was to annex Turkish territory east of Trabzon, a part of Kurdistan, and other areas, with a population of from 2½ to 3 million. However, the wishes of the Russian leaders went farther than that, and had victory been attained, the Russian frontiers would certainly have been pushed deeper into former Turkish territory. Tsar Nicholas, reacting to the outcome of Foreign Minister Sazonov's negotiations with the Allies concerning future annexations, wrote, in the margin of a report of the Russian Ambassador in London: "Agree, except Point One. If our armies reach Sinop, there must be our frontier." The Russian Navy Department was likewise claiming

13. *Ministerstvo Inostrannykh Del. Reformy v Armenii* 1912–14 (Petrograd, 1915).

for Russia a larger area on the shores of the Black Sea, obviously in order to make of the Black Sea a Russian *mare nostrum*.

The Armenians themselves went even farther than the Russian Tsar in their anti-Turkish propaganda, carried out in Europe and America. Their program called for a new independent Armenian state (as opposed to the Russian scheme of outright annexation), extending to the Mediterranean. After the November Revolution of 1917, when Russian Armenia declared its independence, the Armenians dreamed of one great Armenia uniting the former Russian and the Turkish Armenias into one nation. The Armenian program was so popular in 1917 and 1918 that Woodrow Wilson tentatively accepted it in his Fourteen Points. In Point Twelve he declared for "absolutely unmolested opportunity of autonomous development" for non-Turkish nationalities then under Turkish rule. Commenting on the Fourteen Points, Walter Lippmann and Frank Cobb, members of a body of American experts at the Peace Conference, stated that "Armenia must be [given] a port on the Mediterranean, and a protecting power established." [14]

After Turkey's surrender, therefore, the armistice treaty gave the Allies the right to occupy Turkish Armenia. In April, 1920, the Allied Supreme Council invited President Wilson to define the southwestern boundaries of Armenia. His definition was later em-

14. Memorandum on the Fourteen Points, quoted in Harry R. Rudin, *Armistice, 1918* (Yale University Press, 1944), p. 421.

bodied in the peace treaty with Turkey. In November, 1920, he awarded Armenia about 40,000 square miles of Turkish territory; subsequent inclusion of Russian Armenia was foreseen.

All the programs for Turkey's partition contained dynamite for British-Russian postwar relations. This was true not only in relation to the proposed solution of the Dardanelles question. In the Middle East, too, the incorporation of the Armenian territories into Russia would actually mean the creation of the long-expected and long-feared British-Russian frontier. Britain was to take Iraq from Turkey, so that in the north Iraq would probably border on the new southern frontier of Russia. Turkey, which has played a great role during the interwar period from 1920 to 1939 as a buffer between Russia and Britain, would no longer be in existence as an independent nation had the allied war program been realized.

First the revolution in Russia upset the schemes of conquests, with its declaration that the doctrine of "no territorial annexations" would henceforth constitute the highest principle of Russian war programs. What was even more important, Lenin's government had to adhere to this principle so far as Turkey was concerned. Russian military forces were hardly sufficient to reannex Georgia, on the Turkish border, which had declared itself independent in 1918. A war with Turkey was out of the question. The Soviet Government signed a separate peace treaty with Turkey in March, 1918. Moreover, certain Russian territory, including the cities of Kars and Ardahan, had to be ceded to Turkey, so that the future Soviet Armenian Republic was deprived of an important part of its population. This was an unexpected gain for Turkey after her defeat in the World War, and this strip of former Russian land, which still is in Turkey's possession, will undoubtedly play a role in future political relations in the Middle East.

In 1919 the nationalist Turkish revolution under Mustapha Kemal Pasha began. From the angle of foreign policy the revolution was aimed at the Allies, chiefly Britain. It was Kemal's conviction that the prerequisite of a successful fight against Britain was a close alliance with Russia. Such an alliance was also the desire of Lenin's government; every obstacle that stood in the way of it must be removed. An Armenian state was therefore out of the question; Turkish annexations of Russian-Armenian territories in the Caucasus were confirmed.

In the realization of claims to Turkish territories Britain was the only really lucky player among the powers. She acquired, under different titles, decisive influence in vast Turkish lands—Iraq, Palestine, Arabia, in addition to Cyprus and Egypt. Britain's Asiatic empire reached its peak in the '20's and '30's of the present century. During those interwar years the extent of her possessions in the Middle East was greater and the number of her enemies smaller than ever before. The Russian danger in the north had been removed. Although Soviet activity in the Middle East was extensive, the Soviet state itself was weak.

Meantime Soviet Russia had become Turkey's best friend in world politics. Indeed since 1920, she had no friend but Russia. Britain had plundered half her territory; Italy had annexed her islands and, under Mussolini, was building a large navy and openly menacing her; France, somewhat more inclined to friendship, had taken Syria and Lebanon from her. Russia, on the contrary, favored Turkish policy at every step, and the new Dardanelles regime, so favorable to Ankara, was to a great extent brought about by Soviet assistance at the Montreux Conference of 1936. By the Montreux convention Russia, too, acquired important privileges for her navy. Turkey did not forget that Soviet Russia had acquired no Turkish possessions and that Russia's backing of Kemal's government was responsible to some extent for the failure of the British-French-Italian-Greek scheme of partition as well as for the abolition of the Sèvres Peace Treaty.

A reversal, however, did occur in Russo-Turkish relations just as had previously occurred in the relations of Russia with her other southern and eastern neighbors. After the outbreak of the second World War "mutual assistance pacts" between Russia and her smaller neighbors were becoming the favorite diplomatic instrument of the Soviet Government. The granting of military bases to Russia was implicit in all agreements of this kind concluded or contemplated (Finland) in 1939–40. Simultaneously with the dramatic negotiations concerning mutual assistance pacts with the Baltic States—negotiations that eventually led to agreements—Moscow started similar talks with Turkey. Soviet demands were concerned mainly with the Dardanelles and Russian military rights in the Straits.[15] Russian forces at the Dardanelles!—it was an ominous concept for Turkey. The specter of the old Russian Empire was rising out of the Black Sea before Turkey's eyes. Moscow's demands were rejected and so were the mutual assistance pacts. In taking this decision the Turkish Government undoubtedly followed the lead and counsel of Great Britain.

In October, 1939, while Russia was tied to Germany, Turkey signed her treaty of friendship with Britain (and France). Both Turkey and Russia at that time were neutrals. While Turkey's neutrality was pro-British, the Soviet Government collaborated with Germany. The estrangement between Ankara and Moscow was growing steadily.

Turkey, however, found a way of staying out of the war almost to the end, and this caused disappointment to her British ally as well as to the Balkan nations

15. The exact wording of the Soviet demands has not as yet been published. H. C. Wolfe reports (*The Imperial Soviets*, p. 226) that Stalin put this proposal to the Turkish Foreign Minister: "We shall send a Russian garrison to the Dardanelles to protect your territory; we shall establish air and naval bases in the region of the Sea of Marmara to defend your interests." Joseph E. Davies likewise reports, in *Mission to Moscow*, p. 468: "I was told that Russia's demands on Turkey included a military base that would control the Dardanelles similar to those in the Baltic. This is quite possible."

—Yugoslavia, Greece—which had hoped for Turkish assistance against German and Italian invasion. She continued to trade with Germany and supplied her with important raw materials. At the same time she feared German aggression. More than once, blacked-out Istanbul was full of rumors of imminent German advance.

Four days before Germany attacked Russia a new political agreement was concluded between Germany and Turkey. Turkey's relations with Russia remained strained.

This state of affairs did not undergo any substantial change after the German-Russian War began. Britain, having become an ally of Russia, went out of her way to reconcile Ankara with Moscow; on a number of occasions the Soviet and British Ambassadors in Ankara made statements regarding the integrity of Turkish territory; later, lend-lease supplies were allotted to Turkey by the United States Government. In the allied capitals hope prevailed, during 1942 and 1943, that Turkey would join the allies and enter Bulgaria, fight the Germans, or at least grant the allies air and naval bases in the Dardanelles. Moscow was the most interested among the allies and also the most insistent. While British efforts were directed chiefly through diplomatic channels, the Soviet press was openly attacking Turkey for her "neutrality, which serves only the German interests." Russian broadcasts in 1944 reiterated "Turkey's guilt" for great numbers of Russians who had to die because of Turkish neutrality.

On February 23, 1945, Turkey finally declared war on Germany. A few weeks later, the Soviet Government denounced the Soviet-Turkish pact of friendship which had been in force for twenty years, and *Pravda* declared it "outdated."

Behind this portentous move loomed, first, Turkey's new role as Britain's outpost in the Balkans and Middle East, and, secondly, the question of the Dardanelles. When the Big Three powers opened a new discussion with Turkey on this problem—late in 1944—they advanced the idea of the creation of a small state, incorporating the Straits, under international control.[16] This compromise would certainly not be sufficient for the Soviet Government, since the other powers, being in the majority, would be in a position to close the Straits to Russia no matter what the wording of a new agreement might be. The compromise would certainly be contrary to the interests of Turkey. And finally, even if accepted by Britain, it would run counter to her traditional interests; she would prefer to see the Straits in possession of a small power, like Turkey.[17]

"Unless the unexpected happens," wrote Professor James T. Shotwell and Francis Déak a few years ago, "and the war ends shortly, one can be reasonably certain that the question of the Straits will be raised in

16. *New York Times*, November 7, 1944.
17. J. A. R. Marriott, *The Fortnightly*, October, 1944.

one form or another. When and how this will occur it would be dangerous to prophesy; but . . . it is safe to predict that if and when the issue is raised, either during or after the war, we will see Great Britain, Russia and Turkey at the three corners of the triangle . . ." [18]

This prediction is being borne out. It is a natural principle of Turkey's foreign policy that she side with the enemies of the strongest power in the Balkans and in the Eastern Mediterranean. Before 1914 Russia was her chief enemy: during the first World War Turkey sided with Germany. In 1920–25 Britain was the most hostile among the powers: Turkey became Russia's ally. In the late '30's Italy was the chief menace: Turkey looked for assistance to France and Britain. Since 1939, and especially since Italy's defeat in 1943, Russia has reassumed the significance in Turkish eyes that she previously held. With the Balkans occupied by the Red Army, with Russian forces on the Bulgarian-Turkish frontier, with the Black Sea under Russian control, and with renewed Russian activity in Iran and the Middle East in general, Turkish policy turned more and more to British support.

Turkey, like Greece, was becoming an outpost of British power, a balance on the British scale. The Turkish-Bulgarian border in Europe and the Turkish-Soviet border in Asia were becoming, in a way, the Russo-British border.

18. James T. Shotwell and Francis Déak, *Turkey at the Straits* (1940), p. 136.

The Powers in the Middle East

WHAT is true of Turkey is true also in relation to Iran: had there been no revolution in Russia, the state of Iran would not exist today. The partition of Iran was almost accomplished in 1915–16.

During the nineteenth century Iran was of the classical type of Asiatic buffer state. From the British point of view the Iranian and Afghan mountains and deserts were a natural defense line of British possessions, a barricade against aggression on the part of a European power. For Britain's European enemies, however, Iran and Afghanistan were the only road to India. Whether the enemy was approaching from the west, through Turkey, or from the north, through the Caucasus and the Caspian, he had to pass through Iran or Afghanistan. In preparation for his war on India, Napoleon dispatched Count Jaubert and General Gardanne to Iran to pave the way for a military alliance. In 1801 Tsar Paul of Russia moved an army against the British in India, ordering it to go through Turkestan and Afghanistan. Kaiser Wilhelm had the Middle East in view when his policy began to penetrate into Turkey and was gaining influence in Teheran.

Napoleon was defeated, as was Kaiser Wilhelm. Russia, however, not only kept her place but expanded to the south. Unlike Britain, Russia did not consider Iran merely as a buffer state but rather as the next station on the road to power of the Russian Empire. The whole of Iran could fit into the structure of the empire, as had her northern part (with Baku) which had been annexed to Russia as early as 1828.

The northern part of modern Iran, in the vicinity of Russia, is the most populated and most advanced region of the country. The south, on the other hand, is poor. A large part of the territory is desert. Iran's largest cities, including the capital, lie in the north. During recent decades, before the first World War, its trade went to a large extent in a northerly direction, to Russia. Cultural ties existed between Iran and the Caucasus, and even Iran's political evolution followed the Russian pattern. The Russian Revolution of 1905 gave impetus to similar movements in Iran, where a revolutionary outbreak occurred in 1906. The granting of a constitution providing for a *Majlis* (parliament) in Iran followed the opening of the Russian Duma. And then, exactly as in Russia, the revolutionary movements subsided and a counterrevolution won successes. It was Russian military force that defeated the revolution in Iran, the reason being that the government of St. Petersburg regarded an Iranian revolution as a menace and Iran as a field for political and military intervention.

For a certain time during the nineteenth and early twentieth centuries England played in Iran the role of a liberal antagonist of Russian autocracy. At times British prestige in Iran was high. During the course of the Iranian Revolution, however, there was an important turn in Britain's policy. According to the British viewpoint the immediate danger to Britain following Russia's defeats in 1904–5 was Germany rather than Russia. At that time Germany had penetrated into the Near East and a British compromise with Russia appeared more and more advisable.

In 1907 a general Anglo-Russian agreement on the Middle East was concluded. To put an end to rivalry in Iran, the northern part was declared an exclusively Russian sphere, the southern a British sphere. To avoid conflicts and clashes and in order not to create a common frontier, a neutral zone between the two spheres was declared. This neutral zone constituted the last domain of real Iranian sovereignty. The Russian area was large and rich compared to Britain's. Moreover, it was in actuality a direct territorial extension of Russian territory to the south from the Caucasus. On the other hand, Russia recognized the whole of Afghanistan as a British sphere of influence.

Northern Iran was of course not annexed to Russia, nor was southern Iran added to the British possessions. The government of Teheran, although not independent, was still running the country after 1907. Iranian laws, duties, and taxes, and an Iranian police force were in operation. It was evident, however, that one day, when great international upheavals would again take place, outright annexations would be carried out.

The partition of Iran was completed in 1915, during the war. The new British-Russian deal was connected with the secret treaty concerning the Dardanelles. While reluctantly agreeing to Russian demands in Turkey, the London government asked Russian

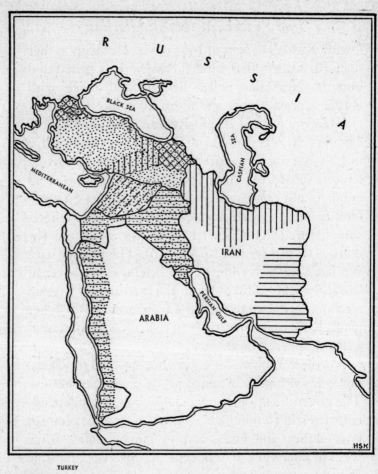

PARTITION OF TURKEY AND IRAN

consent to the extension of the British sphere in Iran to the north, to include the former neutral zone. St. Petersburg acquiesced on condition that a certain improvement in its internal Iranian frontier be allowed.

A common Anglo-Russian frontier inside Iran became a fact; after the war it would have constituted a prolongation of the new Anglo-Russian frontier in Turkey, if the program of the Allies concerning the Middle East had been realized.

The 1917 Revolution in Russia had enormous consequences for Iran. Russian armies departed and the Soviet Government declared its principle of self-determination of nations. Meeting with no resistance, British forces expanded to the north, occupied the whole of Iran (it was another case of nature abhorring a vacuum), and even brought a part of the Caucasus under British influence. In 1918–19 Britain was master of the whole region from Baku to the Persian Gulf.

British successes were far greater than she had ever expected. All of her adversaries—Turkey, Russia, and Germany—were crushed.

But the reaction set in promptly. Under the influence of the Russian Revolution and, to a still greater degree, the Kemalist movement in neighboring Turkey, internal upheavals of a revolutionary character took place in Iran, too. The strong nationalist movement bore all the traits of the great movements in Asia during the '20's: repudiation of international extraterritorial privileges, strong resistance to foreign intervention in Iranian affairs, abrogation of "unequal treaties," and, more important than anything else, liberation of Iran from the domination of foreign armies. In its international aspect the movement was directed, although not exclusively, against Britain.

In 1920 Russian forces again landed on Iranian soil, in Pahlevi, a port on the Caspian. The British withdrew their scanty army from the northern region, which was immediately occupied by Soviet forces. A revolutionary Iranian Government under Soviet occupation was created in Resht, and the Red Army remained in northern Iran for a long time. Only after the withdrawal of the British from the central provinces did the Soviet forces leave northern Iran.

For the British Empire the early '20's was a period of reverses, after the great successes of 1918–20. Events would certainly have meant a catastrophe had it not been for British political instinct which prescribed a quiet and clever retreat from advanced positions. During those years armed interventionist activities in Russia had ended disgracefully, and Britain was withdrawing her forces from Russian soil. The Turks were rising in rebellion against the Treaty of Sèvres and Britain decided not to enforce the treaty by means of her army and navy. Afghanistan struggled for independence, and concessions had to be made. In Iran a great anti-British movement was in the offing, and London decided to evacuate the country, which a short while before had appeared to be developing into a new British protectorate. How sensible it had been for Britain to retreat became obvious after only a decade, when she succeeded in regaining a great deal of her influence in the Middle East.

In 1921 Britain declared at Teheran that she agreed to annul the victory treaty of 1919, but at the same time Iran signed a new treaty with Moscow. By this agreement Russia ceded to Iran all her private and official economic rights: Russian roads and railroads on Iranian soil, oil concessions, cable and telephone lines, port installations, a Russian bank, and so on. Iran had to obligate herself not to cede the former Russian concessions to other foreign groups.

At the head of the revolution in Iran was an army officer, Reza Khan. He climbed the ladder to power rapidly. In 1923 the old Shah fled to Europe and in 1925 he was declared dethroned; a few months later Reza Khan became himself Reza Khan Shah Pahlavi. In 1927 he denounced all extraterritorial rights of foreign lands and foreign subjects. Sweeping reforms accompanied the new international program in family life, the army, education, radio, construction of roads and railroads, and other matters. In a way the movement was kindred to the revolution in Russia. It was, however, entirely free of any Communistic ingredients, and to this fact it owed its rapid successes.

The advantageous position which Russia had achieved in Iran during the early '20's was not maintained.

The nationalist revolution was soon ended. Economic reforms and new construction required capital and active trade, which could come only from non-

Russian sources. The Anglo-Iranian Oil Company was raising its output, and in the '30's Iran advanced to fourth place among the oil-producing nations; the royalties which flowed into the Iranian Treasury from this source were attaining great magnitude. The commercial treaties with Russia left dissatisfaction in Iran; Russo-Iranian trade, very important before 1914, amounted to only $35,000,000 in 1937 and $24,000,000 in 1938 (exports plus imports). During the same two years British-Iranian trade amounted to $68,000,000 and $71,000,000.

Meanwhile, and especially during the '30's, a third power, Germany, was achieving great influence in the Iranian economy. Germany's prestige in Iran was based upon her remoteness from the scene of perennial conflicts with Russia and Britain as well as on her economic resources and abilities. In a sense, German activity in this area was a renewal of the Kaiser's *Drang nach Osten*—an attempt on the part of Germany to create a Middle Eastern empire and to obtain oil for her imminent wars. In the early '30's Germany was seventh among the nations trading with Iran; in 1938 she stood second ($34,000,000). When the European war started, British trade with Iran had diminished. Germany, importing and exporting through Russia, attained first place in 1939–40; and in 1941 her star was shining bright in the Iranian sky.

The spring of 1941 marked the height of German successes in the Middle East. The Balkans had just been conquered, Crete was occupied, and German-Italian armies were advancing in North Africa. The next stage of the war would be played, it seemed, in the Middle East. Turkey, a corridor to the Orient, expected a German attack momentarily, particularly across the Bulgarian border, only eighty miles from Istanbul. The island of Cyprus, a British possession off Asia Minor, likewise awaited a German invasion. It appeared obvious that the oil-rich lands of Iran, Iraq, and Arabia would be the next station on the road of the German march, since Britain was standing alone against the conqueror of Europe, with the Mediterranean closed to her shipping and with almost no war supplies going to the Middle East.

German activity in the lands of the Middle East at that time was extensive and highly successful. In Iran Reza Shah himself (praised in the '20's by the Soviet press as "a far-sighted leader") was the best friend of Germany, and his government followed his line. The German colony in Teheran was growing rapidly and "tourists" arrived in great numbers. In neighboring British-held Iraq a pro-German plot was in preparation; on April 5, 1941, it broke out, and the German puppet, Rashid Ali Galiani, seized power. In India anti-British elements were becoming more and more active. Syria, a mandate of defeated France, was expecting a German invasion. It was, as it were, the eve of a general breakdown of the old empire, with Germany emerging as its successor in the Middle East.

Whether all these anti-British moves were entirely serious on the part of Germany will become known only when German archives are opened. It appears that to a large extent Germany's Middle Eastern war preparations were designed to divert Russian attention from the German armies moving to the Russian borders in Europe; at a later date Hitler boasted that he had succeeded in this respect. Officially Germany and Japan were demanding that Russia join the tripartite coalition (Germany, Japan, Italy) as a full-fledged member in a war on Britain and America. As a reward, according to newspaper reports, Hitler proposed to Stalin a compromise in Asia on the same pattern as their division of "spheres of interest" in Eastern Europe in September, 1939: Iran was to fall into the Russian sphere.

The Soviet Government readily entered into these negotiations. Participation in the war was of course not contemplated, and adherence to the Three Power Pact was not possible for Moscow. But a status of neutrality in Asia in 1941, like a status of neutrality in Europe in 1939, with territorial gains, was exactly what the Soviet Government wanted. It viewed with apprehension the growing German influence in the neighboring Middle Eastern lands, especially in Iran, while its own relations with the Iranian Government grew progressively worse. Its specific method of defense preparations was enlargement of its possessions in the buffer territories.

Soviet armies were concentrated in the Caucasus and Turkestan.[19]

All this diplomatic activity has had no practical results, since Hitler preferred the conquest of Russia to a peaceful division of spheres. The only result for Moscow was an outline for a future Russian sphere in the Middle East, which in many respects coincided with prerevolutionary ideas of Russian expansion in Asia. The scheme was also analogous to the scheme of a great sphere in Europe, from Finland to the Black Sea. Although conceived at the time of Russian collaboration with Germany, it remained a program for the anti-German war, too. A Soviet sphere in northern Iran, which had been a reality in 1907–17, and which emerged as a blueprint in 1941, remained an essential point in the postwar program.

After only a few months in the blueprint stage, the sphere became a reality. What was only an offer on the part of Germany in April, 1941, was becoming a fact in September of the same year. Soviet armies

19. The Japanese press, well informed of events in this part of the world, reported that the Soviet Government had demanded in Teheran the right to occupy northern Iran. The Turkish *Yeni Sabah* reported that "a division of spoils between Russia and Germany, with India and Iran falling to Russia," with Germany receiving permission to use all the oil from the Near East (*New York Times*, May 13, 1941), was being discussed. Other sources reported that the theme of the discussions was division of Iran into two spheres, the southern part to go to Germany, while Russia would be rewarded in Afghanistan.

were moving in from the north while the British were occupying the southern provinces of Iran. A radical purge of all vestiges of German influence was being conducted jointly by the British and Russian armies. The all-powerful Shah was dethroned and deported, and the Iranian Government resigned. The German *Braune Haus* was closed, and hundreds of Germans were arrested or fled the country. Iran was transformed into a great corridor for transport of war supplies to Russia from Britain and America.

The agreement signed by Russia, Britain, and the new Government of Iran in January, 1942, guaranteed the integrity of Iran, both powers engaging to withdraw their armed forces not later than six months after the end of the war. The United States was not a party to this agreement, which had been drafted before America's entry into the war. At a later date, during the Teheran Conference between the leaders of the Big Three (December 1, 1943), America's pledge of Iran's independence was given when the common declaration was signed: "The governments of the United States, the USSR and the United Kingdom are at one with the Government of Iran in their desire for the maintenance of the independence, sovereignty and territorial integrity of Iran." And then came a showdown which, although prematurely, lifted for a moment the veil from the controversial Iranian problem.

Oil concessions play varying roles in the policies of the individual powers toward Iran. For Britain and

America oil is the aim, and political guarantees in Iran are the necessary consequences. For Moscow political prerogatives are the aim, and the output of oil only a secondary element or even only a pretext. For the Western powers oil imperialism means political influence to the extent that this is necessary for the output of oil. Soviet oil policy in northern Iran was motivated not so much by the need for concessions as by the aim of not allowing other nationals to acquire a stake in this potential Russian sphere. The political consequences inherent in a foreign concession, whether it be an oil or a railroad concession, were the factor determining the attitude of Moscow.

Russia is in a position to develop and enlarge her oil output without benefit of foreign resources. Russian oil resources have been variously estimated by experts, but there is no doubt that they are very large. In 1925 the Russian Professor Ramzin estimated them at 37.4 per cent of the world's total reserves. Professor Strizhev has put them at 45 per cent.[20] Recent Russian investigations have arrived at much higher figures. In 1939 the official *Great Soviet Encyclopedia* put the world's oil reserves at 9.5 billion tons, with Russia's at 6.4 billion and America's at 1.8 billion. "As far as oil reserves are concerned," it says, "the Soviet Union occupies the first place, possessing 67.2 per cent of the world's reserves." "Since 1937, all Soviet geologists and economists have maintained that

20. Azmoudeh, *Le Petrole en USSR* (Paris, 1934).

Russia controls more than half of the oil reserves of the world." [21]

These figures are probably greatly exaggerated. The fact is, however, that Russia's reserves would make possible for her a great extension of her oil output and participation in the world oil trade without recourse to concessions abroad. Russia's oil output, which has grown considerably in the last fifteen years, has been absorbed by her industry, transport, and mechanized agriculture. Lack of capital has prevented the expansion which would have been possible, and has kept Russia from playing an important role in the international oil trade.

Since the early '20's the policy of the Soviet Government has been to prevent any deal by a foreign oil company which manifested interest in oil concessions in northern Iran, or, if the concession had already been granted, to prevent its operation. In the latter case it demanded concessions for Russian nationals (on the ground, for example, of prerevolutionary contracts), or created special oil companies (for instance, the Kavir Khurian Petroleum Company). It was prepared to pay large sums of money to the new foreign concessionaries in northern Iran for relinquishing their concessions and leaving the region. This policy was sometimes also applied to other parts of Iran. Thus, several American oil companies have given up their

21. *Russian Affairs* (New York, 1944, No. 3); N. Mikhailov, *Land of the Soviets* (Lee Furman), pp. 20–21; I. M. Gubkin, *Mineral Reserves of the U.S.S.R.*, pp. 15–16.

enterprises (although allegedly for other reasons), for instance, the Amiranian Oil Company and Seaboard Oil Company of Delaware.[22]

Since 1942, when British and American companies began to seek means of expanding the oil output in Iran, the Soviet Government, in accordance with its established policy, began to pay increased attention to Iranian oil. Moscow saw danger in British domination and in the rapid infiltration of American interests in Iran after the war, when the oil companies, backed by their governments and influential because of their wealth, would remain in and around Teheran. The Iranian Government, on the other hand, was most resentful of the Russian projects; it was aware of the political aim behind them. It was afraid of these political implications and was therefore inclined to grant concessions to British and American companies but not to the Soviet Government. Such a policy on the part of Iran was, however, utterly impossible. All these countries were war allies—the armies of the Big Three were present in Iran. Discrimination against one of these governments was out of the question.

On September 2, 1944, the Iranian Government decided, not without consultation with the British, to turn down all requests for oil concessions and, in general, not to grant any new concessions so long as alien armies were within Iran.

The American ambassador in Iran addressed a letter to the Iranian Government on November 1, 1944,

22. *Newsweek*, October 23 and November 13, 1944.

confirming the latter's decision to postpone all talks concerning foreign oil concessions until after the war. His request was that American oil companies be informed when the Government of Iran should begin new negotiations. At the same time the London radio declared that "the British Minister is in close contact with the Persian Government and has no objection to their decision." Thus, there emerged a sort of "united front" consisting of Britain, the United States, and Iran.

The Soviet Government protested vigorously against the decision of the Government of Iran. The Moscow press declared the Iranian Prime Minister Mohammed Said (who had been Ambassador in Moscow for a long time and was considered a friend of the Soviet Union) was "disloyal and unfriendly" to Russia; it suddenly recalled alleged "sabotage" in connection with munitions on Iranian soil intended for transport to Russia. Turning against the forces behind Mohammed Said, *Izvestiya* asked "how the presence of troops of another state [the United States] on Iranian territory" was possible "without any treaty with Iran":

"Apart from Soviet and British troops that are in Iran in conformity with the treaty of alliance, there are also American forces in Iran. These forces stay there entirely without a treaty with the Iranian Government." [23]

Mr. Sergei Kavtaradze, Vice-Commissar for For-

23. *Izvestiya*, November 1, 1944.

eign Affairs, present in Teheran at that time, made statements to the press against the Iranian Government. He was also the driving force behind the newspapers which supported the Soviet request for concessions. "Leftist groups" in northern Iran arranged street demonstrations. In Tavriz, Teheran, and smaller cities, public processions were staged in which thousands of Iranians, poor and hungry, proclaimed as their most important need "oil concessions to Soviet Russia."

Mr. Said, the Premier, had to resign, and *Pravda* was gratified. It was a lesson for the future.

On December 3, 1944, the Iranian Parliament approved a bill prohibiting Iranian officials from negotiating any oil agreements under penalty of imprisonment for from three to eight years. Thus the road was barred to any new concessions to the three interested nations. The consequence was a series of new street demonstrations in the northern provinces, while Sergei Kavtaradze requested the government to suppress five newspapers which were critical of the Soviet demands. The Moscow official *War and the Working Class* wrote that the Iranian law forbidding new oil concessions "is clearly in the interest of securing a monopoly position for present oil concessions in Iran." It concluded with a threat: "The future will show to what extent the ruling circles in Iran are capable of drawing the necessary conclusions."

Since the beginning of 1945 the pro-Soviet party in Iran, the Tudeh (The Masses), has been feverishly

active. The party claimed a membership of 100,000—
a huge figure in view of conditions in Iran. Street
demonstrations took place in Isfahan and Teheran in
April, 1945, at which the creation of a new government was demanded. The leader of the Tudeh party,
Irei Iskendari (a former member of the French Communist party) demanded oil concessions for Russia
and a mutual assistance pact with her.

On April 22 the government resigned. Three days
later the San Francisco Conference opened and the
Iranian delegates obediently followed the Soviet lead.
At the end of May the new government, with Hakimi
as Prime Minister, demanded evacuation of all foreign
military forces from Iran. A few days later it had to
resign, too.

VIII

THE POWERS IN THE FAR EAST

THE UNITED STATES AND THE FAR EAST

TODAY it seems strange, even unbelievable, that only a short historical while ago a multitude of great powers were elbowing one another in the Far East, intriguing, dividing territory, occupying ports, demanding indemnities. The deafening roar which emanated from the Far East at times drowned out all other sounds in international negotiations. It even appeared that the clue to mankind's future lay hidden somewhere in the sands and waters between the Yellow Sea and the Malacca Straits. And then, in a surprisingly short time, these forces were one after another eliminated.

A universal fever of seizure and partitioning of foreign lands, of colonial wars and military expeditions, has, since the beginning of the '80's, affected old empires as well as newcomers in the field of Weltpolitik. Even smaller nations, not equipped for oceanic wars and acquisition of colonies, have been touched by the epidemic. Britain, Russia, and France, of course, stood at the head of the expansion-hungry nations during the '80's. But now even old Bismarck, traditionally continental in his Prussian policy, stretched his hand toward the Pacific and Africa. Italy tried to acquire

Abyssinia, Belgium effected settlements in the Congo. In the short space of two decades, at the most—historically but a moment—the immense continent of Africa was divided and redivided among the European powers.

The fever of empire affected even the American policy of that period. The United States suddenly became active in the Pacific and Caribbean, laying the foundations of a complicated edifice which might be called the American Empire. With the partition of Africa complete, the Far East remained the last great unoccupied region of immense possibilities, trade prospects, railroad prospects: a region of nations with populations in the hundreds of millions, and of weak states—a region in which the old and new empires were able, it seemed, to fulfill their most ambitious programs. Compared to the Far East, Africa was a trifle. Its population was only 20 per cent of that of China, Korea, and the Philippines. A group of powers —Russia, Japan, and the United States—absent in Africa, were very active in Eastern Asia.

France was advancing from the south, from Indo-China; she actually succeeded in creating her own sphere inside China, in the provinces of Yünnan, Kwantung, and Kwangsi, bordering on Indo-China and constituting, in a way, a geographical continuation of her Far Eastern empire. Japan, newly embarked on a policy of conquest, was advancing from the east, through Formosa and Korea. The United States had settled in the Philippines. Germany took archipelagoes in the Pacific and a port in northern China. Even Italy demanded ports and installed a settlement in Shanghai.

Foremost among the powers were, of course, Britain and Russia. Britain was everywhere and advanced along all roads. The greater part of Far Eastern trade was in British hands. The British Ambassador was the chief foreign personage at the court of His or Her Chinese Majesty. Extraterritorial rights were conceded first to Britain. Of the foreign settlements in the Chinese cities, the British were the largest. It was chiefly Britain that educated Japan in Far Eastern matters. She took Japan by the hand and led her, like a child, into the circle of powers. Without British help Japan would hardly have risen to greatness. During the first decade of the present century no arrangement or settlement concerning the Far East was effective if it did not have the approval of Britain.

The pace of Russia's expansion out of the north was rapid and persistent. By the dawn of the new century Russia had succeeded in marking out a special sphere for herself, a sphere huge in area, although not so large in population. Within the span of only a decade there were included in the Russian sphere regions north of the Chinese wall, Mongolia, Manchuria down to the Yellow Sea, enormous lands bordering on the great Gobi desert, and the forests on the Yalu. The Chinese capital, Peking, found itself at the gates of the Russian sphere. Russian influence was growing from year to year. Had a division of China taken place at the beginning of the twentieth century (as was prophesied more than once) Russia would have acquired the whole northern half of China starting at the Afghan frontier and ending at Peking, an area stretching along the 35th or 40th degree of latitude, which in general constitutes the approximate Russian border all over Asia, from the Black Sea through the Caucasus and Middle Asia, and would now be continued up to the Pacific.

"From Port Arthur," Prince Bülow said, "Russia can quietly watch the dissolution of the Chinese Empire."

The Far East has developed in a school of shrewd, cynical, sinister, and, when called for, suave, diplomacy. Slogans and formulas which were widespread in Europe during the years of the first World War and which acquired great importance in the second, were first tried out in the East. The proclaiming of the "sacred principles" of "independence and self-determination" of nations, especially on the part of Japan and Russia, resulted in Korea being swallowed up, in Manchuria becoming a foreign sphere of influence, in Liao-tung being separated from China. So satisfactory were the results of the experiments in the use of these slogans that they were repeated in 1918 by Germany and Austria in Brest-Litovsk, with the aim of detaching the Ukraine from Russia and occupying it. They were employed by Japan, first in Korea, then beginning in 1931 in her campaign to create the state of Manchukuo, and again in 1943–45 by Russia, in her attempt to set up a line of vassal states in Central and Eastern Europe. China, the cradle of a great civilization, became also the cradle of a special system of "friendly international relations."

Another instrument of modern diplomacy—the pact of mutual assistance—has likewise been successfully employed in the Far East in the course of the last fifty years. When China was defeated by Japan in 1895 and was forced to cede important territory, including Port Arthur and Talienwan to Japan, Russia sprang to China's aid, insisted on the annulment of this clause of the treaty, concluded an assistance pact with China—and then claimed for herself, and acquired, from China the very same peninsula, including Port Arthur and Talienwan. "There is no document of modern times," wrote an intelligent and informed observer, concerning this assistance pact between Russia and China, "that has exercised a greater or a more calamitous influence upon the history of the world." He saw in it even a cause of the first World War.[1] Indeed, it became the basis for subsequent Russian encroachment on a large scale. And since those days and down to the 1940's the powers have often employed, in Europe, treaties of assistance and friendship of the kind that had been experimented with in the Far East.

The system of "spheres of influence" was not invented in the Far East, but it, too, was employed there on the most extensive scale. Had there not been such a multitude of competing interests, China would have been definitively divided into foreign spheres several

1. W. H. Ouderdyk, *Journal of the Royal Central Asian Society*, 1935.

decades ago. The very multiplicity of interests was her salvation at that time.

Since 1915 one great power after another has been eliminated from the Far East. Germany was the first to lose her privileges and possessions. Before the first World War had ended Japan was firmly entrenched in the German-held archipelagoes north of the equator, and Chinese ports were cleared of every vestige of German influence.

After 1918 Russia, militarily weak, was an object, not a subject, of Far Eastern great power policies. Only through the Chinese Communist movement and the Kuomintang was she able to exert a certain influence on Chinese affairs. She had to remain aloof from her former sphere in Manchuria, and to share with China control over the Chinese Eastern Railroad, which was eventually sold to Japan. Only Outer Mongolia, the least important part of the old sphere of the empire, remained under Soviet tutelage.

France made no attempt to expand in the Far East after the first World War, especially since Germany's resurrection in Europe. From 1940 to 1944, of course, the French Vichy Government had to follow the German lead and the French possessions fell into the Japanese sphere. Even after her liberation in 1944, France, although resisting Japan in Indo-China, remained too feeble to play any active role in the great events of the Pacific.

Between the two World Wars even Britain did not retain in the Far East the position she had previously held there. She was gradually developing into a cautious and hesitant force in the face of the enormous energy displayed by rising Japan. While the European powers were slowly backing out of China, Japan was moving into the vacuum via the "Twenty-One Demands" of 1915, secret treaties with the Entente, the Lansing-Ishii agreement of 1917, the Paris Peace Conference, the occupation of Vladivostok and Siberia, and the Washington agreements of 1921–22.

Nor was England in a position to play a great role in Pacific affairs during the new World War. Defeated by Japan in 1942, preoccupied in Europe, and resisting successfully only in India and Australia, Britain lost for all time her dominant part in the Far East. Her enormous investments in Chinese industry disappeared, and no postwar indemnities will be able to restore them. She no longer is the leading nation in the trade with China, and she is not likely to recover the position. Britain's prestige has suffered enormously. She will take part, of course, in the final settlement of Eastern affairs, but she can do so only as an ally and "junior partner" of the younger great power—the United States.

Thus, all the great European powers have been partly or entirely eliminated from the Far Eastern struggles. The fate of the Far East is being decided in a struggle between two powers, one Asiatic, the other American. If Japan loses, America will succeed—so it may seem—to the role of guiding nation in the greatest area in the world.

But another Asiatic power, emerging as though from a long faint, again displayed military strength and influence—the Soviet Union, possessed of a peculiar policy, its intentions indiscernible, and with a mysterious program for the East, began to come to the fore in the 1940's, thus disputing the future one-power predominance of the United States. Can this be taken to indicate that an entirely new two-power system of activity in the Far East is appearing? What is the essence of the new American and Soviet policies in this cauldron of world affairs?

TWO AMERICAN CONCEPTS

Looking back at fifty years of American Far Eastern policy, one wonders whether it was a farsighted political investment from which advantages could be expected to accrue in the future, or a quixotic policy dealing in idealistic phrases, declarations of principles with no force behind them and no intention to translate them into action. Was American Far Eastern policy a unique display of wisdom or was it actually an absence of policy? There is no middle ground between the two extremes. History has not yet pronounced judgment. The trial is in progress, and the world will know the result in the near future.

From the beginnings of American Far Eastern policy until the weeks before Pearl Harbor, two different American concepts and two open door policies alternated and overlapped.

The one had sharp anti-imperialistic features. It

strongly advocated the independence and integrity of China; it was in favor of abolishing unequal treaties, privileges for the great powers, foreign occupation of ports or territories, spheres of influence, foreign armies on Chinese soil. In this respect the United States was alone in the crowd of nations. Although opposed to the policy of all powers in China, this course of the United States was particularly antagonistic to the most aggressive among them. At times it was Russia, at other times Japan.

America's anti-imperialist trend in China sprang from different sources. In the main it was the outcome of the experience of the American people themselves, liberated through bloody wars from the yoke of foreign imperialism and still exalting every nation's fight against oppression. It was a result also of America's fabulous economic prosperity which made the trade with China and investments in China less important for her than for other nations. It was also the outcome of America's military weakness; her navy was inferior to the British and more distant than the Japanese; her armies were so far away from the Far Eastern scene that their force could not impress Britain, Russia, and Japan, who in all debates concerning Far Eastern politics presented heavy arguments in the form of battleships, artillery, and infantry. The immediate practical results of America's policy were therefore negligible. The authors of the policy could comfort themselves only with the hope that a time would come when their long uncompromising fight for the independence of

China would suddenly bear rich fruit, that in a political world liable to constant change America's principles were seeds which needed decades in which to grow into majestic plants. In this sense the policy of the United States may have been perhaps the most far-sighted and the most ambitious of all modern policies. The deeper purpose behind it may even be the inclusion of the whole of the Far East, with its half billion population—about 25 per cent of the people of the world—into the American orbit, not through conquest of the Asiatic peoples but through opposing the numerous foreign masters of these peoples. In this sense the objectives of American policy were not a few muddy ports, not some particular railroad concession, but the whole of great China.

The other line of American policy was quite the opposite: it called for immediate positive achievements. It is difficult to carry out a policy in the way that a farmer might plant forests for the benefit of his grandchildren; in politics it is not usual to calculate profits that will accrue only after long decades. At times the United States questioned the usefulness of constantly opposing the powers in the Far East when these powers persisted in their policies and were obviously approaching a partition of China. What is the sense of preaching morality to incorrigible amoralists? Does not America make herself ridiculous by doing so? America must howl with the wolves, must descend from the skies to the mundane realities and be like other imperialist sinners. How often have presidents, secretaries of state, and public leaders, tired and desperate, ended up in retreat, in a return to the paths of "realism!" During such attacks of practicality American leaders have proceeded along the well-known roads: they have insisted on opportunities for investment of American capital in railroad concessions in China; they have struggled for facilities for American trade; they have recognized the establishment of foreign spheres in Chinese territory; they have even demanded Chinese consent to American occupation of Chinese ports, as was done by Germany, Japan, Britain, France, and Russia.

The formula of the open door had to cover both systems of American policy. As a slogan of realistic businesslike policy, the open door implied admittance of American trade into any port of China occupied by other nations. By implication it was even a kind of American consent to foreign encroachment on Chinese territory: if you Germans occupy Kiaochow, you will have to sanction our right to do business through this port; if you Japanese take southern Manchuria, you may not shut the door to American business. Equal rights for all nations in the exploitation of China! Equal opportunity for trade! In this sense the open door has been an old principle, often advocated and applied by the British. It had, however, another meaning, too. Sometimes the open door policy has been enlarged and interpreted so that it was synonymous with the integrity of China, the recognition of true Chinese sovereignty over the whole of Chinese territory, and the granting only of trade facilities to the trading nations. The underlying concept was the elevation of China to the status of the independent nations of Europe or the Americas. For this purpose the doors of China had to be opened to foreign goods and investments as the doors to trade had been opened in Spain, Portugal, Brazil, or Argentina, that is, to permit economic activity without political privileges.

BACK AND FORTH

IN ONE of his famous open door notes, John Hay, Secretary of State, proclaimed, in plain words, the guiding idea of American policy in the Orient: the independence and integrity of China. "The policy of the government of the United States," he wrote in his note of July 3, 1900, "is to seek a solution which may bring about permanent safety and peace to China, preserve Chinese *territorial and administrative entity,* protect all rights guaranteed to friendly powers."

Only a few months after this note was written, the American Government decided to demand a separate port in China, just as the British, French, Germans, and Russians were doing at that time. The demand, however, was not pressed and did not lead to any practical results.

When Russia violated the integrity of China in 1903 by including Manchuria in the Russian sphere, Theodore Roosevelt had either to fight or to accept the action as a *fait accompli*. He decided, of course, to adopt the second course. His Secretary of State, Hay, wrote: "I take it for granted that Russia knows as we do that we will not fight over Manchuria, for the simple reason that we cannot."

The author of the open door notes was not the only American statesman to arrive at this discouraging conclusion. A similar evolution had occurred in the thinking of many an American leader who had had charge of Far Eastern affairs: first, lofty principles, then disillusionment, then compromise. When, finally, Theodore Roosevelt himself took over the handling of Far Eastern questions [2] he appears to have started where Hay had begun in 1899, and then, ". . . within three or four years he fell back to the position to which Hay had been forced to retire: the American people simply would not support a policy of intervention in Asia." The American Ambassador Edwin Conger, having arrived at the same conclusions, gave most striking expression to them in his letter to the Secretary of State, in words of despair which retained their force for a long time, perhaps even until today:

"What's the use? Russia is too big, too crafty, too cruel for us to fight. She will conquer in the end. Why not give up now and be friendly?"

In 1903 Britain invaded Tibet and sought to create a kind of protectorate over this Chinese province. The Department of State immediately opposed the move and demanded that the Foreign Office confirm that it does not intend "to disturb the present government of Tibet or lessen Chinese control over it." (June 3,

2. Tyler Dennett, *John Hay* (New York, 1933), pp. 403–410.

1904). Meantime, Japan was emerging victorious from her war with Russia. Now Roosevelt asked the Japanese Government to confirm that it "adheres to the position of maintaining Open Door in Manchuria and of restoring that province to China." Likewise, the American-Japanese treaty of November, 1908, proclaimed the "independence and integrity of China." Meantime, the original ardor had abated and Roosevelt was becoming more and more "realistic."

In a memorandum presented by him to the newly elected President Taft, Roosevelt summarized his long experience in Far Eastern affairs in words of sorrow: "A successful war about Manchuria would require a fleet as good as that of England plus an army as good as that of Germany. Open Door policy in China was an excellent thing . . . but the Open Door policy completely disappears as soon as a powerful nation determines to disregard it and is willing to run the risk of war." Therefore—Roosevelt meant—many of the integrity-of-China declarations made by the United States were mere gestures with nothing behind them. But, Roosevelt said, "I do not believe in our taking any position anywhere unless we can make it good." "Never draw unless you mean to shoot."

In 1907 a net of new international agreements defined the various spheres in China, in disregard of American principles and policies. Britain, Russia, France, and Japan were rounding off their spheres. In 1911, before the fall of the Chinese dynasty, Britain, Russia, and Japan managed to acquire rights, respectively, to Tibet, Mongolia, and Manchuria. The American Government was unable to prevent this development. Again reverting to its more modest concept, the State Department (in May, 1912) even recognized that a foreign government might use "such protective measures" within its sphere "as may be forced by necessity." [3]

Even Japan's aggressive policy against China during the World War, starting with the famous Twenty-One Demands, did not cause the United States to revert to its policy of more idealistic political concepts. "The United States frankly recognizes," William Jennings Bryan, the Secretary of State, informed Japan in March, 1915, "that territorial contiguity creates special relations" between Japan and the territories of her sphere. The principle of "contiguity" is the basis of most of the "sphere" and "zone" concepts. In the case of China the principle, if recognized, would lead far.

The typical countermove to Japan's demands on China occurred two months later, when Bryan in a note stated that the United States "cannot recognize any agreement or undertaking" between Japan and China which would impair "the political or territorial integrity of the Republic of China or the Open Door policy."

Both types of United States principles were applied to the economic sphere in China, especially to the mat-

3. E. B. Price, *The Russo-Japanese Treaties of 1907–1916 Concerning Manchuria and Mongolia* (Baltimore, 1933), p. 72.

ter of railroad construction. Railroads were foreign strongholds; a railroad concession to a foreign syndicate was often tantamount to the granting of a sphere of political interest. Partition of China was proceeding by means of the consummation of agreements between the Chinese Government and foreign syndicates. The American idea was expressed at times by attempts to buy off the railroads and to concentrate them in the hands of an international company, in order to remove the imperialistic implications of the concessions. The attempts were unsuccessful. They were followed by a reversal in American policy to an official tendency to maximum participation of the United States in the railroad syndicates. No striking progress in this direction was achieved either.

In 1917, in the course of American-Japanese negotiations, Secretary Lansing included in his draft of an agreement the provision that the United States and Japan "will not take advantage of present conditions to seek special rights or privileges in China," and stated that both nations are opposed to special rights or privileges of other powers which "would affect the independence or territorial integrity of China." At the conclusion of the negotiations, however, Lansing signed a document setting forth the principle of "territorial propinquity," and recognizing "that Japan has special interests in China, particularly in the part to which her possessions are contiguous."

At the Paris Peace Conference President Wilson and his group struggled against difficult odds when

202

they tried to support China. The years from 1918 to
1922 were a time of extremely strained relations between the United States (over racial equality, Yap,
naval rivalry, Siberia, and so forth) and Japan, and
American support of China's independence constituted one of the difficulties. In his program for the
Pacific (Washington) Conference, Charles Evans
Hughes referred to the guarantee of the integrity of
China as an essential point in this program.

In the meantime the "integrity of Russia" had become an issue, too. The armed intervention in Russia,
under way since 1918, provoked on the part of the
United States the same uncertain policy as in the case
of China. Two policies were possible in dealing with
the Japanese invasion of Russia. The one would be a
war against Japanese aggression in the name of the
"integrity of Russia." Was there available, however,
the force necessary and the willingness to fight Japan
if this had to be done? If not, a second road was open:
to revert to a "realistic policy," take part in the military intervention in Russia, and then neutralize and
counterbalance the Japanese influence.

The American course wavered between the two
policies. First there was a half-hearted intervention
which did not achieve its aim of neutralizing Japanese
influence. It was followed by the early departure of
the American troops before the Japanese left. Other
methods, involving international pressure on Japan,
led to the ending of the Japanese invasion. This was a
rare occurrence in Far Eastern history.

As far as China was concerned, the wavering in policy continued. The Washington Conference (1921–22) adopted a resolution pledging its members, including Japan, "to respect the sovereignty, the independence and the territorial and administrative integrity of China," and even "to refrain from taking advantage of conditions in China in order to seek special rights or privileges." However, many of the "special rights and privileges" acquired by Japan during the World War were retained by her, especially those in Manchuria. In connection with these, Secretary Hughes emphasized the "realistic issue" of equal opportunities for all trading nations.

While the '20's on the whole marked a period of relative—of course only relative—calm in China in so far as the great powers were concerned (Britain and Japan even renounced certain of their privileges there), the beginning of the '30's heralded a new storm. In 1931 Japan invaded Manchuria and in subsequent years widened her zone there. The American Government was again faced with the old dilemma: a protest that would be ineffectual, or acquiescence and trade?

In January, 1932, the State Department stated, in its notes to Japan and China, that it does not recognize "any situation *de facto*," nor does it intend to recognize any agreements which impair "the sovereignty, the independence or the territorial and administrative integrity of the Republic of China."

In a letter approved by the President and published

in the press in February, 1932, Secretary of State Stimson described the past and the present United States policy in the Far East as a constant fight for China's integrity and sovereignty. "The program for the protection of China from outside aggression is an essential part of any such [orderly] development. The signatories and adherents of the Nine Power Treaty rightly felt that the orderly and peaceful development of the 400,000,000 of people inhabiting China was necessary to the peaceful welfare of the entire world." [4] No action, however, was taken to support these principles. In 1933, when President Franklin Roosevelt took office, his first acts evidenced a return to compromise with Japan and virtual, though not actual, recognition of the new Japanese Empire on the continent.

"I believe," Cordell Hull informed Japan, "that there are in fact no questions between our two countries which . . . can be regarded as not readily susceptible to adjustment by pacific processes. It is the fixed intention of the American Government to rely . . . upon such processes." The government will be prepared, Hull said, to examine Japan's position "in a spirit of amity and of desire for peaceful and just settlement."

Nevertheless the conflicts with Japan became more tense during the '30's. The League of Nations' investigation of the Manchurian question, Japan's withdrawal from the League, her departure from the Naval

4. Henry L. Stimson, *The Far Eastern Crisis* (New York), p. 172.

Conference in 1936 and her refusal to participate in naval limitation on the proposed bases, and finally her war with China, which began in July, 1937, made the possibility of agreement between Washington and Tokyo more remote. The Roosevelt government, however, was ready, more often than not, to effect a compromise. It constantly sought a basis for agreement. The American military force stationed in the Far East was negligible. The extensive trade with Japan during the years just preceding the war was a continuation of the old, "practical," "realistic" policy. The official diplomatic support of China's integrity remained the textual policy.

Because America's Far Eastern policy was lacking in that unity and singleness of purpose which were characteristic of Japan's policy earlier, and of Britain's, its achievements were insignificant. The American concept of the integrity of China had won a certain amount of sympathy for the United States in nationalist China. No other power had, even in words, gone as far as America in championing China's independence. A vague possibility of a future alliance of the United States with China was the sole and somewhat meager result of that policy.

In the field of practical economic policy the achievements were no greater. In 1930–35 America's trade with China represented only 3.5 per cent of the total American foreign trade. Of the $12,630,000,000 of American investments abroad in 1935, only $132,000,-000, or approximately 1 per cent, was invested in

China. "Americans owned a mere 6 per cent of the total foreign investments in China in 1931, as compared with Britain's 36 per cent ($1,189,000,000) and Japan's 35 per cent ($1,136,900,000)." [5]

Only a war could demonstrate the practicality of the policy of integrity and sovereignty of the Far Eastern nations. America was not prepared to wage major wars for the sake of these principles, nor was she prepared for a major war in general. "Never draw," Theodore Roosevelt said, "unless you mean to shoot." His successors often did draw, but without success, since the world was certain that they would not shoot.

The shooting was started by Japan, in December, 1941, and now America had to wage the great war which she had striven for four decades to avoid. Now the greater of the American concepts in relation to the Far East suddenly became real. Integrity of the Orient and peaceful collaboration among its nations became a program of the war, first, because the other powers had previously been eliminated from the Far East; second, because the defeat of Japan would eliminate the most persistent of the powers in Far Eastern aggression; and third, because a war requires idealistic slogans and lofty ideals. Compromise may be expedient at the peace table; wartime ideology, however, calls for unconditional realization of the biggest of programs.

5. A. Whitney Griswold, *The Far Eastern Policy of the United States* (New York, 1938), p. 469.

Accordingly, the Cairo Conference of the Far Eastern allies—the United States, Britain, and China—in December, 1943, adopted a program for the Far East which enunciated that "Japan shall be stripped of all the islands of the Pacific which she has seized or occupied since the beginning of the First World War in 1914; all the territories that Japan has stolen from the Chinese, such as Manchuria, Formosa and the Peskadores, shall be restored to the Republic of China. Japan will also be expelled from all other territories which she has taken by violence and greed . . . In due course Korea shall become free and independent."

Such a program seemed quite natural. If Japan were defeated she would of course lose all her possessions on the continent as well as the islands which were formerly Chinese or German. China's sovereignty over all her former lands would be restored. However, neither these aims nor stability in the new relationships in the Far East could be accomplished merely by the defeat of Japan. Russia was again becoming a great power in the Far East and her policy was acquiring a growing influence in discussions of future settlements.

RUSSIA AND COMMUNISM IN CHINA

THE revival of certain schemes and programs of old Russia in Soviet policy has an important bearing on the situation in the Far East.

During the two decades preceding the revolution, Russian policy built up a sphere of influence in China and the Far East; for geographical reasons it was natural that the northern part of China and Korea should constitute the territory of the proposed or the created sphere. Manchuria was included in it at the end of the last century but the southern part of it was lost after the war with Japan. Outer Mongolia was made a Russian protectorate in 1912. The agreements concerning railroad concessions actually gave Russia an even greater territory—the whole region north of the Great Wall. (The approximate extent of the Russian spheres is seen on the map, page 211.)

After the November Revolution the Soviet Government in part renounced and in part lost its spheres of influence in the Far East except for Outer Mongolia. Another large Chinese territory—Sinkiang (Chinese Turkestan)—was falling into the Soviet sphere in the '30's. This vast although thinly populated province is separated from China proper by the Gobi desert; connections between Sinkiang and Russia, although leading through the Pamir and the Altai Mountains, are easier than between this province and China proper, and a new Soviet railroad which runs close to Sinkiang, opened in 1930, has strengthened the ties of this area with Russia. In the late '30's Sinkiang's economy was under Soviet control, its army was headed by Soviet officers, and the frontier from Sinkiang to China was carefully watched. Recently, however, these ties have weakened.

The most important components of the old Russian sphere in the Far East have fallen into Japanese hands: Port Arthur and southern Manchuria, in 1905; Korea, around 1910; the southern part of Sakhalin, after the Russian Revolution; and the rest of Manchuria in 1931. Russian penetration into the East was not checked by a China growing powerful. Japan, Russia's rival, was becoming the dominant power in Asia, the successor of the Russian and other "spheres," and therefore the antagonist, actual or potential, of every power in the Far East.

The difference between the situation in Europe during the war with Germany and the situation in the Far East is the great military and economic weakness of the main continental force of the anti-Japanese coalition. Unlike the warring nations of Europe, China has been torn by civil war which has been going on for the last fifteen years. Neither Chinese party has been strong enough to defeat its rival. While the government of Chiang Kai-shek is probably representative of the majority of the people, its power has not been decisive. Although the Chinese Communist Government, a strictly warlike organization best adapted to battle, has command over a militarized population, it is not able to defeat the force of the Central Government. This state of affairs is bound to become an issue of serious importance in the near future.

The peculiarity of the Chinese Civil War is its territorial aspect. The first "Soviet regions" in China emerged in the south immediately after the break between the Communists and Chiang Kai-shek, in December, 1927; they were liquidated, however, the fol-

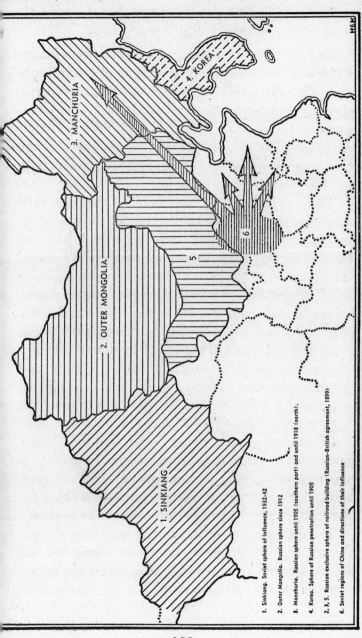

1. Sinkiang. Soviet sphere of Influence, 1932-42

2. Outer Mongolia. Russian sphere since 1912

3. Manchuria. Russian sphere until 1905 (southern part) and until 1918 (north).

4. Korea. Sphere of Russian penetration until 1905

2, 3, 5. Russian exclusive sphere of railroad building (Russian-British agreement, 1899)

6. Soviet regions of China and directions of their influence

RUSSIAN SPHERES IN CHINA AND KOREA

lowing year. In 1930 new areas were occupied by Chinese Communists. These were held more firmly than were the earlier regions, and in February, 1930, the first Provisional Soviet Government was established in the western part of Kiangsi province, with Mao Tse-tung as its leader. A few months later the first Congress of the Soviet Regions took place secretly in Shanghai.

This was actually the beginning of the great civil war which was mainly centered in the relatively industrialized, richer, and more populated parts of China—the territories between Nanking and Canton. This location of the Soviet regions was natural, since the Communist movement arose in China, as everywhere, in the East, among young intellectuals, students, and to a lesser degree, workers, in the larger cities. Soviet China had to live and fight in the vicinity of the great ports, between the British, French, and Japanese spheres, inside or near the "international settlements," attracting the attention and arousing the fears of representatives of all the great powers.

In January, 1934, a second Congress of the Chinese Soviets took place in Juichin, Kiangsi province. It was reported to have drawn eight hundred delegates and, what was more important, to have welded together in one semi-state six scattered Soviet regions.

The government of Chiang Kai-shek several times dispatched armies against the Soviet insurgents, but the expeditions were not able to suppress the movement altogether. A Chinese Red Army was created in 1928. According to its own, probably exaggerated, reports, it numbered 10,000 in 1928, 62,000 in 1930, 175,000 in 1932, and 350,000 in 1934. It was a kind of guerrilla army, capable of moving swiftly when in danger.

In 1934–35 there occurred the great transplantation of the Soviet regime and its army from the southeast to the north of China, over a distance of thousands of miles. The full significance of this transplantation, which was an event with profound implications for international relations, was not recognized at the time.

The Chinese Red Army, the active component of the Chinese Communist movement, together with the state machinery of the Soviet areas and their military organizations, began their long march in the fall of 1934. It was an exploit involving battles, hardship, and heroism. The army moved first to the west. Reaching the border of Yunnan province, and uniting with other Red forces, it turned to the north. Then it began a new march of thousands of miles, arriving finally at the provinces of Shensi and Shansi, almost at the Mongolian border, where, at the end of 1935, it settled down. The new region became the center of the new Chinese Soviet state.

The motives behind this great march were twofold. First, the forces of the Central Government were growing stronger and it was becoming evident that the next expedition against the Soviet regions would end in the annihilation of these relatively small island-states of Chinese Communism. Second, Japanese aggression in the northeast, which was already under way at that time, threatened not only China but Soviet Russia as well. Manchuria was occupied in 1931. Subsequently the occupation was extended to other provinces. The Japanese threat to Russia was growing, and a great war involving the three states simultaneously seemed to be in the cards. Under these circumstances the Russian Soviet Government needed the assistance of its loyal Chinese ally. No other means of collaboration between the Russian and the Chinese Soviet forces was possible than through a transfer of the latter to the corner of China nearest to Russia and at the point where the Japanese front begins. This corner of China has been finally chosen as the center of the new Chinese Soviet state.

Since the removal of its center to the north, the activity of the once more growing Chinese Communist movement has been in the sphere of military and external policies rather than in revolutionary transformations on its own territory. The new Soviet region is extremely poor peasant land, having no industry, no foreign trade, and no real capitalism. The "social revolution" was limited by force of circumstances to reforms in taxation and education, and to reductions in land rents. A new administration was set up, with modest salaries to officers. According to reports, the traditional bribery of officials was eliminated; this was less difficult to accomplish here than elsewhere, since the active party in every affair of bribery—the rich—were few even before 1935 and were becoming even fewer after the settlement of the Communist armies in the region.

The main preoccupation of the new Chinese Soviet authorities was the creation of an army, after the heavy losses suffered during the Grand March. The army expanded rapidly again. Its main activity was, of course, the civil war with the Central Government, which continued. Following a study of Russian and Western European methods, new advisers and military leaders were added to the old, and the production of war weapons was started in the few poorly equipped shops which were created in the Soviet state.

Direct frontal activity against the Japanese was not possible. What seemed more important to the leaders was the penetration of the Chinese towns and villages behind the Japanese front line—the great hinterland, where the forces of Japan and of the pro-Japanese puppet governments were feeble—where small pro-Soviet kernel groups were organized, and a sustained contact with Yenan, the new Communist capital, established.

The Soviet region has often been defined as a state within a state. It was more than that. With its separate territory, government, army, money, and military insignia, it grew rapidly to the status of a real state—another state of China. The number of its original population was perhaps comparatively small—it was a few million at the most. The movement spread, however, and soon claimed control over tens of millions of Chinese in the neighboring Japanese-occupied territory.

The Big Three

The Chinese Soviet state had become an important force even before the outbreak of Japan's war against China in 1937. Its importance grew still more after that date.

SOME MISCONCEPTIONS

STRANGE misconceptions concerning Chinese Communism which are widespread in the United States are frequently the source of erroneous political conclusions. Communism in China, some say, is moderate and not inclined to revolutionary activity but contents itself with progressive reforms: in a word, it is reformist rather than revolutionary. Communism in China, others contend, is not a part of Moscow's network; unlike all other Communist parties, it was and is independent of any outside influence and represents merely a Left wing in the public opinion of China.

In reality, however, the Chinese Communist party is a loyal member of the Communist family, devoted to its head and ever ready to carry out instructions. It is "revolutionary" or "reformist" in the same sense as are all other Communist parties, employing maneuvers, zigzags, and changes in slogans as circumstances require. Chinese Communism has had its struggle with dissident factions; its Trotskyism, denounced as pro-Japanism; its "Right deviation"—denounced as "pro-imperialist"; its purges; its civil war tactics, derived from Russian tactics. The "reformist" zigzags were often dictated by Moscow, and the Russian influence has sometimes been the moderating factor in the pol-

icy of Chinese Communism, which otherwise would
have followed a more revolutionary course that would
certainly have been detrimental to it. On the whole,
there was never a disciple more obedient to a teacher
than the Chinese Communist party. This state of affairs did not change after May, 1943, when the International was officially dissolved.

The Russian party has stood by since the birth of
Chinese Communism, namely, since its second party
Congress in 1922. The "Chinese question" was one of
the issues which forever separated Stalin and Trotsky; their struggle revealed many important facts. The
Russian Politbureau, the real government of Russia,
was deciding the fate of the Chinese party, and the
Comintern had only to put its signature to the decisions
of the Russian leaders. Stalin's moderate tactics (to
instruct the Chinese Communists to remain inside the
Kuomintang party), dictated by the poor prospects
of a fight against the great powers in the Far East, were,
in Trotsky's eyes, a betrayal of Communism. So they
seemed, too, to the majority of the Chinese Communists. But once adopted in Moscow, the instructions
were followed in China and resulted in the loss of only
a minority of the party, who either withdrew or were
purged. In 1930 Trotskyites even succeeded in winning for a few months leading positions in the Chinese
Politbureau. They were soon accused by the Stalin
faction of premature creation of collective farms and
preparation of an armed insurrection against the government of Chiang Kai-shek, when it was obvious that

the revolt would be crushed. In January, 1931, the Chinese Stalinists, backed by the powerful authority of Moscow, finally and permanently drove the Trotskyites from all leading posts. The struggle against Trotskyism continued, however, until the '40's; it appears that Trotskyism was stronger in China than in Russia.

Even apart from this factional struggle, the ties between Russian and Chinese Communism were of the closest possible nature. The Executive Committee as well as the Congresses of the Comintern devoted much of their attention to China. Documents published in Moscow in 1934 [6] contain over forty resolutions and excerpts from decisions taken by the highest bodies on the course of Chinese Communist policies. The Chinese party, advanced during the '30's, after the collapse of German Communism, to first place in the long row of national Communist parties—excluding, of course, the Russian.

In Moscow the attention given to Chinese affairs was enormous, especially after the revolutionary events in Shanghai in 1925. Was the delayed world revolution coming through the East rather than the West, as had previously been expected? Hopes and doubts provoked passionate debates in Moscow. China stood high on the agendas of all deliberating bodies. The Communist Academy founded a special section for Chinese studies. The Moscow Chinese University,

6. *Strategyia i Taktika Kominterna na primere Kitaya* (Moscow, 1934).

named after Sun Yat-sen, obtained Karl Radek to head it. Radek wrote a book on Chinese history, and Stalin studied the details of China's geography and policy. Great hopes were put in young Chiang Kai-shek, Sun Yat-sen's pupil, who studied in Moscow in 1923–24.

Chinese Communism reciprocated this interest. It glowed with veneration of Russian Communism in general and of its leaders in particular. Stalin's speeches were studied as a bible, and the *History of the Communist Party of the Soviet Union*, written under Stalin's guidance and partly by him, was immediately (1939) translated into Chinese and became the main source of Communist knowledge.

In 1935, at the last Congress of the Communist International, the Chinese party was hailed. George Dimitrov, world-secretary of the Communist International, praised the Chinese and declared, "We approve the initiative taken by our brotherly Communist party of China." The Chinese delegate, Wang Min, reported to the Congress that his party would uphold its former decision to increase the numbers of the Red Army in China to 1 million and to extend the Chinese Soviet regions to include a population of 100 millions.

"The growth of the Communist party in China," he said, "is explained by the fact that it works under guidance by the Leninist Communist International, that it is able to make use of the experience of all sections of the International, especially of the section of the Soviet Union."

He especially hailed Stalin:

"Our party is true to the teachings of the man who, after Lenin's death, has further developed the theory and the tactics of Marxism-Leninism; of the man who has theoretically elaborated the basic strategy and tactics of the Chinese revolution—to the teachings of the great Stalin."

Three leading members of the Chinese party—Mao Tse-tung, Wang Min (Chen Shao-yui), and Chang Kuo-tao—were elected members of the Executive Committee, and Wang Min was elected a member of the Presidium, which remained in office until May, 1943. One of the three, Chang Kuo-tao, was purged in 1938 by the Comintern, and Mao Tse-tung declared him "dogs' dung below human contempt."

In his message of greeting to the 18th Congress of the Communist party of the Soviet Union, in 1939, Mao Tse-tung said, speaking on behalf of Chinese Communism:

"We are certain that our great country will achieve its victory just as you have attained a victory unique in history. Long live Comrade Stalin!"

At that Congress Spanish Communism was the chief recipient of praise, but the Chinese party was by no means forgotten. Manuilsky [7] reported that membership in the Chinese party had reached 148,000. "The Communist party of China," he said, "has accumulated the experience of a Soviet movement, of building a

7. Dmitri Manuilsky was the Russian member of the Secretariat of the Communist International. At present he is Foreign Commissar of the Ukraine.

Soviet Government, and of a great guerrilla movement."

In September, 1939, Mao Tse-tung declared in an interview (at a time when even the Communist world was shocked by the Stalin-Hitler pact) that outside the borders of the capitalist world "there exists another, a bright world—it is the Soviet Union. The Soviet-German pact has raised the international significance of the USSR . . . Friendship with the Soviet Union must be strengthened in order to effect the joining of the two great nations."

These declarations and demonstrations were taking place at the very time that American writers and reporters were insisting that Chinese Communism was a separate movement, not tied up with Russia and independent of Moscow.

The most recent and most important phase of the Soviet movement in China began in 1936–37 and continues to the present. It almost coincided with the period of the war between China and Japan. During this period the ties binding the Chinese Soviet Government to the government in Moscow have remained strong. Only in this way could the Chinese party preserve itself.

In 1936 Japan concluded the anti-Comintern pact with Germany, obviously directed against Russia. In 1937 Japan attacked China. She was certain that the war would be won within a year at the most. Preparations for further operations, also against Russia, were under way. In fact, in 1938 and again in 1939, wars of short duration, but on a high scale of military technics, were waged against Russia in the Far East. Japan was not successful but the danger for Russia remained great.

Under these circumstances Russia needed the assistance not only of Soviet China but of the Central Government as well. Soviet Union policy in China was developing, as has always been the case, along two courses: first, along normal diplomatic roads, leading from the Foreign Office in Moscow to the government of Chiang Kai-shek; second, through the relationship with the insurgent Chinese Communist Government. In 1937–40 Soviet policy was rather a policy of appeasement of the Chinese Central Government and of collaboration with it.

In August, 1937, six weeks after Japan's invasion of China, the Russian Government concluded a non-aggression treaty with the Chinese Government. The protracted negotiations concerning military supplies were secret; supplies of goods began to move from Russia to China somewhat later. These goods were transported across vast distances, over the deserts and mountains separating Russia from China proper. The province of Sinkiang, which was the main corridor through which these goods passed, was actually controlled by Soviet authorities. Russian collaboration with China and a warlike antagonism toward Japan lasted until 1940–41.

A concept of collaboration with Chiang Kai-shek

was incumbent upon the Chinese Communists, too. A rapprochement between the Communists and the Central Government occurred. The new trends in Communist nationalist policy, which were guided by Moscow, had been in evidence since 1935. Chinese Communism was the first among the fraternal sections to enter upon the patriotic, nationalist road; the new slogans and political tactics were first experimented with here before they were applied in Europe and America. As a matter of fact, most of the new Communist policies in Europe which puzzled the world in the years that followed were first applied in China. Thus, a scheme of strategy was ready when the invasions in Europe began.

The new concept made considerable change necessary: nationalist phrases rather than class war formulas; an appeal for national unity in the struggle against the fascist invader; proposals of collaboration made to non-Communist parties on condition that they "really fight the enemy," virtually submitting to the Communist leadership; democracy as the title for this kind of coalition; denunciation of "traitors of the people," who are prepared to "assist the invader," and hatred for and death to all of them; a guerrilla war, urged, organized, and headed by the Communist party behind the front lines; the postponement of the program of social transformation in favor of immediate war needs, and consequently, denunciation of the impatient revolutionary elements such as the Trotskyites, and emphasis on their role of "agents of Japan";

systematic avoidance of the use of the words "Soviet," "Red," and "Communism," and renaming of institutions, organizations, armies, in order to make the terminology acceptable. All these changes had already taken place in China, when Europe was amazed to see analogous developments in France, Yugoslavia, Poland, Greece, and the other occupied nations.

As was the case in Europe, the purpose of these new tactics and maneuvers was, above all else, to enhance political power. While preaching democracy, the Chinese Communists were not really inclined to relinquish an ounce of the power they already held. Their activity was actually directed at the strengthening of their own positions; they were organizing guerrilla groups in the occupied zones. Although not able to fight the Japanese forces (except perhaps in a limited war of sabotage) these guerrilla groups struggled with both the Chinese collaborationists and the guerrillas of the Central Government. As was the case later in France and Yugoslavia, the underground movement in China favored the Communist groups; in the areas of Japanese occupation and Chinese puppet administration a large network of coördinated, centralized guerrilla groups, led by Communists, engaged in constant, bloody conflicts with the other Chinese forces.

In a series of declarations, counterdeclarations, secret and open negotiations, newspaper editorials and official comments, the Chinese Communist party professed to be the most ardent proponents of national unity; the party called for a united nation, a representative national assembly, and amnesty. One factor, however, in these declarations and programs was not mentioned—the Communist armies. The Communists offered to recognize Chiang Kai-shek as supreme head of all the military forces, but the separate armies of the Chinese Soviet Government must not be disbanded, reorganized, or put under direct command of Chungking. Acquiescence in such a condition was out of the question for the Chinese Central Government. Seven years of negotiations involving the question of the Chinese Red Army brought the parties not an inch nearer to agreement.

Beginning in the middle of 1940 Russo-Japanese relations improved. Molotov stated this in his report of August, 1940. Negotiations were leading toward eventual agreement. Japan's military operations were now being directed to the south—Thailand, French Indo-China—and Russia felt more secure than she had.

At the same time the unceasing conflicts between the Chinese Red Army and the forces of the Central Government became aggravated. A large-scale battle took place between them at Moulin in January, 1941. Since that time no real improvement in the relations of the two parties has been noticeable although negotiations were attempted from time to time. Finally, the Central Government imposed a "blockade" on the Soviet regions—actually a front line guarded by a numerically strong Chinese Army.

The Russian Soviet press began to discuss Far Eastern problems in new tones. After 1943–44 it appeared more and more certain that Japan would lose the war; that a Japanese menace to Russia would cease to exist; and that now China, not Japan, presented the greatest problem in Soviet policy in the East. The attitude of Moscow toward Japan was becoming more daring. In a speech of November 6, 1944, Stalin declared Japan to be an "aggressor." Finally, in April, 1945, the Soviet Government denounced its neutrality treaty with Japan. The treaty, concluded at a time when Japan was strong and dangerous, was no longer necessary to Moscow; to have a nonaggression treaty with a Japanese Government at the moment of its downfall would harm Soviet prestige. In 1945 the only possible rival to Soviet Russia in Asia appeared to be the United States with its ally Chiang Kai-shek. The new task was to weaken the ties between Washington and Chungking, to isolate Chiang and to supply arms to the Chinese Red Army.

The attitude toward Chiang Kai-shek began to stiffen. The main accusation made by Russia against him was the same as that used in the propaganda of the Chinese Communists, and essentially the same as the Soviet contention regarding the émigré governments in Europe, namely, that they do not really want to fight the invader; they are not able to organize the underground army and the war industry. Chiang Kai-shek, was the contention, is surrounded by pro-Japanese elements; they do not really want to fight; they would prefer a surrender. The conclusion was that only a combined government, including the Communists—something in the nature of a Tito-Subasitch coalition—could save the situation.

Attacking Chiang for his blockade of the Soviet regions, *War and the Working Class* wrote, in July, 1944: "Marshal Tito's army numbers 300,000, that of Generalissimo Chiang Kai-shek, 3,000,000. Yet the successes of the Yugoslav People's Liberation Army are evident, while this cannot be said of the army of the National Government of China."

The United States was supporting the policy of appeasement of Moscow and, consequently, also of Chinese Communism. Vice-President Henry Wallace made a trip to China in the summer of 1944; en route he stopped in Russia for a few weeks for preparatory negotiations. His insistence upon an agreement between Chungking and Yenan appeared to result in a certain success, and soon negotiations were started between the two Chinese parties. They broke down, however, in December, 1944, since the Communists demanded not only some of the leading posts in the government but, more important, the right to maintain their separate army.

On the insistence of Washington, negotiations were resumed in January, 1945. Chiang Kai-shek proposed a compromise which would have accorded legal status to the Communist party and included Communists in a reshuffled government, but which also called for "reorganization" of the Communist armies. On the other hand, the Communists demanded abdication of the Kuomintang as the majority party and preservation of their Red Army. Chiang was prepared to make further concessions, as, for instance, putting the whole of the Chinese Armies under an American general. The proposals were rejected and, on March 1, 1945, Chiang declared that no agreement had been reached.

The political struggle again burst into the open. A Communist statement accused Chiang of "indulging in gangster talk" and demanded termination of his regime. "He spoke like a lunatic," when he suggested that an American general be placed in command of the armies. This was a veiled appeal to the well-known antiforeign sentiments of the Chinese leader.

The American Ambassador, Patrick J. Hurley, having urged and supported the negotiations, had to draw the logical conclusions and declare that no war material would be shipped from the United States to the Chinese Communist armies. He was convinced, however, that the Chinese Communists are "democratic" and "desire a government for, by and of the people." In April, 1945, he went to Moscow to seek a compromise, but with no success. The Soviet press, in accordance with the Chinese Communists, was accusing Chiang Kai-shek's regime of being the cause of China's defeats and misfortunes.

The rift between the coalitions—Washington-Chungking and Moscow-Yenan—was never deeper than in the spring of 1945, at the time of Germany's defeat.

The Powers in the Far East

It is of the utmost importance to the postwar situation that the northern Chinese regions in the neighborhood of Russia are those where the Chinese Communist resistance organizations are the strongest. In the last several years, however, they have extended their area of activity farther, into the provinces of Shantung, Hopei, Jehol, Chahar, northern Kiangsi, and Honan. Thus there is great probability that the north and northeast of China will, after the war, come under the Chinese Soviet sphere, and that the capital will be transferred from small provincial Yenan to Mukden or Shanghai, or perhaps even to beautiful old Peiping.

A sharp distinction is being made in methods of applying Soviet foreign policy as between countries populated by Russians or other Soviet nationalities, and those lands in which alien groups are in the majority. Eastern Poland, for instance, with her Russian-Ukrainian population, was included outright in the Union; a large part of Bessarabia was simply attached to the Soviet Moldavian Republic. On the other hand, in Yugoslavia and in Poland proper, a technically independent state, friendly to Russia and governed by its own nationals, has been created.

As far as the end result is concerned, no fundamental difference exists; the ultimate aims may be the same in both cases. The distinction is adhered to, however, by Stalin as one of the most important features of his system of solving national problems. It will be strictly adhered to in the East, where Soviet policy must avoid the slightest outward resemblance to the policies of conquest practiced by Japan, Britain, Germany, and old Russia—policies which were resented and hated by the peoples of the Orient.

The Soviet Union, or, technically, the Russian Soviet Republic, does not make extensive claims, territorial or otherwise, in connection with Eastern Asia. Rights of transit through Manchuria to Vladivostok, the return of the southern part of Sakhalin and a few smaller islands, and perhaps some correction of the frontier line, are all that Russia can claim. As far as China is concerned, Soviet ideology rejects any conquest of her territory. Russia will certainly adopt the slogan of a "great and independent" China, on condition that China be controlled by a "friendly government." Such a friendly Chinese Government would offer Russia the use of the naval base at Port Arthur, guarantee her the use of the Manchurian railroads, immediately conclude a mutual assistance pact, and become involved in the large Soviet economic plans. As a reward, the Moscow government can return Outer Mongolia to the Chinese Soviet Government (Chinese sovereignty over Outer Mongolia was recognized by Moscow) and support its claims to a Japanese indemnity. It will also support it militarily in its conflicts with Chungking, which may receive Anglo-American support.

The northern part of China thus becomes an exclusive Soviet sphere of influence. Viewed in historical perspective, this would mean the continuation of the old Russian expansion in China, a major attempt to reacquire possession of previously Russian spheres and to broaden and widen these spheres. How far to the south these spheres would extend depends on the relationships between the world powers. Granting the giving of a certain amount of assistance by America and Britain to the Central Chinese Government, this scheme implies the partition of China between the great victors of the second World War.

The two traditional tendencies of American Far Eastern policy have once more become vocal at the end of the war years: the tendency toward advocating the territorial integrity of China, and that toward compromise with the other powers at the cost of Chinese integrity. In the '40's, however, the two policies assumed new forms and were expressed in new formulas.

Compromise with the other powers in China no longer implies agreements with France or Germany or even Britain. Application to the new situation of the prewar "realistic policies" means compromise with Communist China, as an agent of Russia.

No less than a future partition of China between Russia and the United States (or between Russia and the Anglo-American powers) is the implication of this policy. The pressure put upon Chiang Kai-shek since the middle of 1944 to conclude, at any price, an agreement with the leaders of Soviet China; the insistence upon a coalition government which would include the Soviet party; the acclaim accorded the Chinese Communist leaders and their guerrillas for their alleged military talents; the exaltation of their social reforms; the disposition to accept all conditions imposed, even those demanding a separate army, in order to achieve an agreement with Yenan—all this attracts and breeds forces which will not cease to exist when the war is over. The Chinese forces are, of course, not able to defeat Japan; she can be beaten only by the great powers. But when the day comes that Japan has to abandon Chinese territories, the network of Communist organizations will be strong enough to fight the forces of Chiang Kai-shek; they will strive ruthlessly to occupy as much of the liberated territory as possible. According to the Chinese Communists, the population of the territories under their rule, mainly in the occupied areas, numbered 90 millions at the beginning of 1945, and their army about 500,000 men; they claim a membership of 1,200,000 in the party at present. The Chinese Soviet forces will be supported, of course, by the Russian Soviet Government.

Many rosy reports about conditions in Soviet China have been published lately; they give a biased picture of the stern political system, after the Russian model, under Chinese Communist dictatorship. The criticism of conditions in Kuomintang China may be nearer to the truth, and all citizens of Western civilization would welcome thoroughgoing reforms. However, whether the Chungking course of domestic policy is or is not accepted; whether the criticism which has been made of Chiang Kai-shek's course is or is not justified; whether the Communists in China do or do not represent a progressive movement; whether the atrocities committed in the long civil war were or were not inevitable—none of these questions are decisive for the future course of foreign policy in the Far East. More important is the fact that the Chinese Soviet Government, its state, and its army, gravitate toward Moscow, while Chungking, its state and its army, have an American-British orientation.

Viewed objectively, that is, independently of the wishes and viewpoints of the persons involved in the drama, the compromising line of American policy in China, if it appears again, will lead to a division of the Chinese Republic and to a closed door in its northern half. Granting a compromise solution and the demarcation of new spheres inside China, will this fiasco of the open door policy be accepted by the people of the nation which has steadily advocated this policy in the Far East? Will the Chinese people really take the "First Partition of China" as final? Is it a durable solution, or a short-lived compromise with ensuing new conflicts?

Russia's territorial expansion in China would create a situation similar, in more than one respect to that of forty-five years ago, and with all its consequences. The reëmergence of Japan as a buffer and ally in the witch knot of Far Eastern relations becomes probable. She may be needed by Moscow to offset Anglo-

American pressure. She may also be desired by America and Britain, tired and unable themselves to cope with the unending conflicts in the Far East.

This would not be exactly what the anti-Japanese coalition was fighting for. But another solution would only be possible in one of the following two cases: first, if America were prepared to reject any compromise concerning China and not only fight against Japanese conquests but also uncompromisingly oppose Chinese Communist intervention; second, if Russia would voluntarily renounce any far-reaching designs on China and Korea.

So long as both these preconditions do not exist—and they are absent at present—the decades-old struggle in the Far East will not end on the day that the triumphant American and Chinese Armies sign the armistice with Japan.

IX

RUSSIA AND THE UNITED STATES

IN recent years it has become the fashion to depict Russian-American relations during the last century and a half as pre-invested with harmony—as if a mysterious force drew these two nations together, and Providence itself watched to see that no war arose between them. In this view of Russian-American relations, historical truth and science have often been ignored. In political schemes, biased study often replaces objectivity in order that the desired conclusion may be arrived at; in the case of Russian-American relations the desired conclusion is that in the future, as in the past, everything will be all right. According to this school of thought, only friendly relations between the two powers are historically possible.[1]

1. See for instance: DeWitt Clinton Pole in *New Europe*, September, 1941; Pitirim Sorokin, *Russia and the United States*; to a certain degree also William T. R. Fox, *The Super Powers*, in the same category is *The Road to Teheran*, by Foster Rhea Dulles, and a series of articles in the daily press.

Although much new and important material concerning Russian-American relations has been accumulated both in this country and in Russia during the last several decades, and although it is possible to draw from their history important deductions applicable to the future, a comprehensive analysis of the nature of these relations is still a task of the future. A precondition of any prognosis concerning future Russian-American relations is an objective and unbiased approach to the history of the past and to the present situation.

The Big Three

A study of Russian-American relations may divide the history into two periods: the first, from the War of Independence until about the end of the nineteenth century—approximately 120 years; and the second, from the beginning of the twentieth century to the present.

During the long epoch from Washington to McKinley the United States did not appear as a great power in world politics. Nor was she a great power during the last decades of the nineteenth century. A great nation is not ipso facto a great power. America's armies were small and her navy obsolete. Her political aims being consciously limited to the Western hemisphere, she did not encounter Russia either in Europe or in Asia. Alaska—the "Russian America"—was never a field of important political developments. Since trade between the United States and Russia was also small there was, in fact, no continuity in the course of their relationship, no inner unity, no direct line of development. Their relations were rather a mere reflection of their relations with other powers.

In the foreign policy of the United States during that period first place was occupied by Britain; then followed, in the order of their importance, France, Spain, and Portugal. These four Atlantic nations were in a sense the Atlantic neighbors of the United States. Russia was, by force of circumstance, relegated to one of the last places in the international system of the United States. In the foreign relations of Russia the most important place belonged to Britain; then fol-

lowed Prussia, Austria, France, and Turkey. In relation to Britain, however, the American lines met the
Russian. During the nineteenth century Britain was
the great adversary of Russia and at times an antagonist of the United States. It was therefore the anti-
British policy of Russia and America that brought
these two nations from time to time together. In general, however, there was no uninterrupted line of development, no real *system* of mutual relations. Decades
passed without event, the American and Russian em-
bassies were places of unperturbed quiet. In diplomatic language, relations of this kind are referred to
as "friendly" and even as "good." Occasionally an
unexpected event disturbed the apathy of the diplomats and for a certain time Washington and St. Petersburg manifested interest in one another—only to part
soon again, each to travel its own path.

In deference to Britain Russia did not recognize the
United States during the early years of the latter's
history. It was not so much the revolutionary origin
of the new state as the shadow of London which kept
Catherine II from offering such recognition to the
special envoy from America who was cooling his heels
in St. Petersburg. It was almost thirty years before the
Russian Government recognized the young republic.
When it did, the move was motivated by the relations
of both nations to Britain. Russia found a means of
rapprochement with the United States when, after the
Treaty of Tilsit, she became an ally of Napoleon and
an enemy of Britain. The United States was likewise

237

going through a bitter conflict with London. Recognition of the United States, which occurred in 1809, represented an act of anti-British policy. In his draft of instructions to the first Russian envoy to the United States, Tsar Alexander wrote, in 1809, "I am looking toward the United States as a sort of rival to England."

After several years of wars, and following Napoleon's downfall, there began the significant period of Russia's advance to supremacy on the continent. Russian policy, pursued throughout the world through the channels of both the European Congresses and the Holy Alliance, prescribed suppression of revolutionary movements and consolidation of monarchies; it was a reactionary policy, but coming after a period of twenty-five years of bloody war, it was based on the deep desire of the peoples of Europe for stable, peaceful relations between nations. Suppression of political movements which could provoke international conflicts was in part to serve that end. The grim traits of the Russian policy and the shadow that Russia cast over the world could be tolerated for a certain period by peoples who had suffered through the "world wars" of those times.

Russia's territorial annexations, at the conclusion of the Napoleonic epoch, were extensive, but her influence reached far beyond her new frontiers. It extended to the German countries; to France; even to Spain, where the influence of the Holy Alliance was forceful. The revolt of the Spanish colonies in America against the motherland naturally found an adversary in the Russian Government and its Holy Alliance. The United States viewed as a menace the operations of European powers in the Western hemisphere and therefore was eager, both for sentimental and political reasons, to recognize the independence of the Spanish colonies. Russia, on the contrary, saw in the anti-Spanish movements a threat to peace and legality. Among the motives behind the Monroe Doctrine, opposition to the policies of the Holy Alliance (and her *spiritus rector*, Russia) was a decisive one.

In the Pacific Russia seemed to have become an overwhelming force. While Britain's gradual expansion in the Orient had not yet been felt in the Far East, Russian colonies had reached to the Hawaiian Islands, and plans were discussed involving the Philippines, Haiti, and certain regions of China. On the American continent Russian colonies had begun to move toward California. A great Russian Empire in the North Pacific, including possessions in both the northern part of America and Asia, as well as in the strategically important Pacific islands—such was the Russian dream at the beginning of the nineteenth century.[2]

In 1818 it was fear of possible Russian reaction that restrained the United States Government from rec-

2. "The northern Pacific had to become 'inland waters' of the Russian Empire. This aim implied further strengthening of Russia's position on the western shores of North America, including California, on the Hawaiian Islands . . ." In the view of Minister Rumiantsev (1803) the Russian colonies in America would make it possible "to extend the influence to the East and West Indies"; the expansion was to reach Batavia and the Philippines. Okun, *The Russian-American Company* (Moscow, 1939), pp. 49–50.

ognizing the independence of the South American republics. In 1819 Russia proposed that the United States join the Holy Alliance. The advice was not followed. In 1822, in defiance of the Holy Alliance, Washington finally recognized the South American republics. The Tsar, in a diplomatic note to the American Government in 1823, expressed regret that the United States had seen fit to recognize revolutionary governments. The wording of a subsequent Russian note was even stronger. John Quincy Adams described it as "an exposition of principles relating to the affairs of Spain and Portugal in a tone of passionate exaltation at the counterrevolution in Portugal and the impending success of the French Army in Spain, an 'Io Triumphe' over the fallen cause of revolution, with sturdy promises of determination to keep it down." Two weeks after this Russian message, President Monroe read to the Congress of the United States his famous statement declaring that the United States could not view European intervention in Spanish America "in any other light than as a manifestation of an unfriendly disposition toward the United States." [3]

The Tsar was not frightened by the Monroe declaration, Bailey recounts, he even "was the ruler most likely to undertake intervention. Early in 1824 he appears to have given some thought of doing so. But

3. On Russia, the Holy Alliance, and the Monroe Doctrine see B. P. Thomas, *Russo-American Relations 1815–67*; T. A. Bailey, *A Diplomatic History of the American People*, pp. 180–187; S. F. Bemis, *A Diplomatic History of the United States*, pp. 202–211.

lacking assistance from the other Powers, he soon abandoned any such plans," since "the British navy could not be laughed aside." Indeed, Russian military intervention in America was out of the question, and Monroe's declaration did not lead to any conflicts. Eventually trade treaties were concluded, and there began a long interval of uneventful years in Russian-American relations.

For amateurs of historical analogies, an interesting parallel could be drawn between the pro-Russian peace societies in America at the time of the Holy Alliance, and the Communist sections of the Moscow International in our own times. The Holy Alliance exercised a strong ideological influence through its ideas for a lasting peace and its moral-religious propaganda, and this influence was felt in America. Some thirty peace societies emerged after the Vienna Congress among the states from Maine to North Carolina. They conducted correspondences with Russia and even received a communication directly from Tsar Alexander, who promised to employ his power in order to secure for all nations "the blessings of peace." They published the *Friend of Peace* (Boston) and other material. The movement was of some importance. John Quincy Adams, however, was inclined to view the peace societies as a sort of "fifth column" engaged in "un-American activities." "If our Peace Societies," he wrote in 1817, "should fall into the fashion of corresponding upon the objects of their institution with foreign Emperors and Kings, they may at some future day find themselves under the necessity of corresponding with attorney generals and petits juries at home." He had no faith in Alexander's peaceful aims. Referring to the correspondence between the Reverend Noah Worcester (Massachusetts) and Tsar Alexander upon the blessedness of peace, Adams wrote: "The venerable founder of the Holy League is sending five or six ships of the line, and several thousand promoters of peace armed with bayonets to Cadiz, and thence to propagate good will to man elsewhere . . ." [4]

Ten years after the Monroe declaration a serious conflict over the Polish question arose between St. Petersburg and Washington. (It is interesting to note how frequently the Polish question has played an important role in Russian-American relations.) Not only the American press in general but the *Washington Globe*, considered a semi-official organ, reacted with strong indignation to the Russian methods of suppressing the Polish uprising in 1832; in this it shared the feelings of England and France. The Russian envoy in Washington dispatched a strongly worded diplomatic protest to the United States which charged President Jackson with encouraging abuse of the Tsar. The conflict between the State Department and the Russian Foreign Office dragged on for a few months and ended, as conflicts of this kind usually end, with regrets, suggestions, and hopes expressed by both parties. The incident left the impression of solidarity— today one would say "an ideological united front"

4. John Quincy Adams, *Writings,* VI, 280–281.

—of Britain, France, and the United States in respect to all-powerful Russia.

Then for twenty years again no great events stirred the sluggish course of American-Russian relations.

THE SECOND HALF OF THE NINETEENTH CENTURY

A NEW situation arose after Russia's defeat in the Crimean War. Russian military and territorial losses in this war were not important, but Russia herself ceased to occupy the dominant place among the continental powers; her influence in international affairs diminished; the Holy Alliance was dead. Russian intervention in foreign countries appeared improbable. This situation served to facilitate American collaboration with her. The fifteen years following 1856 were a period during which the relations between the two countries were of the best.

For a long time after the Crimean War Britain and France remained antagonistic to Russia, and more than once it appeared that a new war would break out. Britain and France were likewise the main adversaries of the United States during the latter's Civil War. Britain openly supported the Confederacy and France had embarked on her Mexican campaign. Both were opposed to the Union and were prepared to recognize the secession. The United States therefore welcomed Russian assistance against France and Britain. At the same time the British-American controversy was of great aid to Russian policy.

The rapprochement between America and Russia during the 1860's was, in a way, a political collaboration; the motives were political and not at all ideological, although public opinion drew parallels between the Russian liberation of the serfs (1861–63) and the American war for abolition of slavery during the same period. In a way this thinking bears a similarity to the theory fashionable in our time that the 1941–45 military alliance of America and Russia was an alliance of "democracies." Actually the political systems of the two countries were as different in the 1860's as they have been in the 1940's.

"The United States constitutes a menacing counterweight to England," the Russian captain, A. Popov, wrote in 1859. ". . . there does not exist a state in the whole world more feared by England than the United States." During the American Civil War Russia rejected propositions made by London and Paris in favor of immediate recognition of the Confederacy. "Russia alone," Count Gorchakov, the Russian Foreign Minister, told Bayard Taylor, the United States Ambassador, "is supporting you from the very beginning and will support you in the future." And Lord Palmerston, the British Prime Minister, recognized, in March, 1862, that the menace of a Russian-American alliance had forced Britain to adopt a more cautious course in her dealings with the parties to the American Civil War.

However, the personal sentiments of the Russian leaders were not at all favorable to the cause of the

Federal Government. The Russian envoy reported to Minister Gorchakov that if the North were victorious it would have to resort to "military occupation" to coerce the South and to keep it within the Federation; this, he said, would be the end of American democracy—a turn for the better. "The revolutionaries and the demagogues of the old continent," he said, "have always found moral support and often also material help in the American democracy. With the downfall of the democratic system in the United States they now lose one of their main supports . . . In this respect the American revolution, let us hope, will serve as an instructive lesson to the European anarchists and phrasemongers." At this point in the report Tsar Alexander made a marginal remark: "I would wish it, but I doubt whether it will be so."

Coincident with the American Civil War there also occurred the second Polish insurrection. Again Britain and France were almost ready to wage a war against Russia over the Polish issue. In May, 1863, they addressed the Government of the United States proposing a common *démarche* of the three nations in St. Petersburg in favor of the Poles. The French Emperor appealed to the "historical sympathies of the Americans for the Poles." Had the Government of the United States acceded to this request, serious consequences in relation to Eastern Europe might have resulted. The United States, however, declined to participate in the proposed action; involved in a hard war, she rejected the proposal for an anti-Russian step which might be of assistance to the Poles but which would be unfavorable for her own war. (Again, the analogy with the American attitude toward the Russian-Polish conflict in 1943–44 is striking.)

With the American public, whose sentiments during the war were at a high pitch, the Russian-American rapprochement reached its high point when squadrons of the Russian Navy suddenly arrived in New York and San Francisco in October, 1863. Rumor had it that the Russian Navy would participate in the fighting on the side of the Northern states; that Russia would see to it that there was no intervention on the part of England or France; that she would fight as soon as the Confederate states were recognized by a foreign power. The American newspapers printed leading articles entitled "The Manifest Destiny of America and Russia." "The Meanness of the Western European Powers," "American Alliance with Russia against France and England," and so forth. The Russian naval officers traveled through New England, and the banquets given for them were demonstrations of enthusiasm: "God bless the Russians" was a popular phrase. Half a century elapsed before the real reason for the dramatic voyage of the Russian Navy in 1863 was revealed. It turned out to have had nothing to do with American problems. The reason behind its arrival in America was the danger of a new war over the Russo-Polish question. After her heavy naval losses in the Crimea, Russia feared a similar fate for her Baltic and Far Eastern squadrons; she decided to place her navy at a really neutral base from which it would be able, if war came, to put freely out to sea and to harass British trade. Since the war with Poland did not materialize, no answer can be given to the question whether the Russian idea was or was not a good one. The incident of the visit of the navy, however, exerted a deceptive influence on American public opinion. Actually, the navy had been instructed to take no part in American affairs, and the ovations and banquets tendered the officers were, strictly speaking, not earned.

It is interesting that precisely this historical *quid pro quo* has remained in the people's memory as a proof of the "predetermined harmony" in Russian-American relationships. A recently published Russian study covering the history of this period [5] refers to this concept as a legend and gives a detailed account of its development.[6]

The second outstanding event in the history of the relations between the two countries during the 1860's

5. M. Malkin, *The Civil War in the United States and Tsarist Russia* (Moscow, 1939).

6. In his *American Foreign Relations*, W. F. Johnson says, too: "Russia's ships did not come to our ports at a crucial time, but after the crisis was past, danger of intervention was over, and the triumph of the Union was practically assured." Vol. II, p. 46.

In general, the importance of Russia to the United States during the period of the American Civil War has often been greatly exaggerated. A Russian reviewer has recently compiled a list of works on American history which make no mention at all of Russia in the sections dealing with the American Civil War; the list includes such authors as Charles and Mary Beard, J. R. Hosmer, J. B. McMaster, Woodrow Wilson, James Rhodes, Charles Thompson, Bucles Wilson, and others. A. Efimov in *Krasnyi Arkhiv*, 1936, No. 3.

was the Alaska deal. Two circumstances impelled the Russian Government to decide to get rid of its American colony: the first was an economic reason; the second, the exigencies of the political situation after the Crimean War.

Alaska had been exploited by the Russian-American Company since 1799, but, beginning in the 1840's, the business went badly and large deficits accumulated. The company would have become insolvent had it not had the assistance of the Russian Government, which needed and used the business for other of its designs in the Siberian Amur region and for exploration in China. As a purely business enterprise the Russian-American Company was ready for liquidation long before 1867. The company at the outset had great ambitions. Alaska was only a first foothold for an Empire in the Pacific. However, this dream did not materialize. Alaska was too far away from the heart of Russia to serve as a base of operations. The Russian Navy was inadequate to protect it; Russian trade was inferior to the British and American. Britain, France, and Spain dominated the Pacific; even in Alaska the influence of the rival British Hudson's Bay Company was making itself felt.

After 1856, when the British coalition defeated Russia in the Black Sea, it began to be clear that Alaska was no longer safe for the Russian Empire. In the event of a new war—and the danger of a new war with Britain was real in the 1860's—Alaska could not be defended against Britain's superior navy.

"In case of a war with a naval power," Grand Duke Constantine, the Tsar's brother, wrote in 1857, "we are not able to defend our colonies." In order not to lose Alaska to Britain, he proposed to sell the territory to the United States. This would, in his opinion, provide an amicable solution of a question, "which otherwise will be solved against us, and at that by military means."

The Russian envoy in the United States was instructed to begin negotiations. These were, however, soon interrupted by the Civil War. Meantime, London, the capital of the fur trade, was displaying great interest in the activities of the nearly bankrupt Russian-American Company, which held monopoly rights in Alaska; London was proposing long-term loans on condition, however, that Alaska not be sold to the United States. The Russian Government refused to give such a guarantee. After 1865 Russian negotiations with Washington were resumed and an agreement was arrived at in 1867.

"The impossibility of keeping the colonies in case of a war," the recent Russian work by Okun, summarizing Russia's motives in the Alaska deal, states, "the impossibility of defending them even in peacetime after the rumors had spread concerning the presence of gold in Alaska; inevitable conflicts; and, finally, the transfer of the main Russian interest to Asia—these were the factors which moved the Tsar's government to sell Alaska." [7]

7. *Ibid.*, p. 234.

These urgent reasons impelled the haste manifested by Russia in selling Alaska and explain the ridiculous price of $7,200,000 [8] paid for a territory of great strategic significance which, although thinly populated, was as large in area as Germany, France, and Spain combined, and which possessed important mineral riches (these were, to be sure, only partly known at the time of the purchase). For Russia, with her annual revenue of about 400,000,000 rubles ($270,000,000) a year the $7,000,000 (after deduction for bribes paid by the Russian envoy to members of Congress and newspaper editors) was of no great importance. In the United States the Secretary of State, William Seward, was one of the few persons who comprehended the important role that Alaska would play in America's future wars and policies.

Again uneventful decades passed during which relations between America and Russia were neither bad nor good. During this period each played only a minor role in reciprocal schemes of international relations.

A new chapter in Russian-American relations began around 1900.

Ancient history in Russian-American relations, so to speak, comprised the period prior to 1855—the period when America was a small nation, while Russia was in a position of superiority in continental Europe, with ramifications of policy which extended far be-

8. Russia was prepared to sell Alaska even for $5,000,000 if the United States insisted.

yond the continent, even to America and the Pacific. Medieval history in Russian-American relations was the period between the Crimean War and the end of the nineteenth century: America had grown but she had no world policy; Russia's expansionist policies were confined mainly to the Near East and Asia. The modern history of Russian-American relations, which has been wholly different from the previous periods, started with the advancement of the United States to the rank of a great power and Russia's growing activity in the Far East. This period embraces the four or five decades following the Spanish-American War.

Only during this last period did there develop a real organic relationship between the two nations. Now their political activities were pulsating with unabating vigor. Now the interests of each of them became part of a world-wide political web; now they were meeting one another almost everywhere. During this period no year was uneventful in their relations. Previously, having granted full recognition to one another, and their official agents and agencies being well established, no real political relations, either good or bad, had marred a long sequence of quiet years. Now, on the contrary, events crowded upon one another even during the period (1918–33) when the two nations did not officially recognize one another. This state of affairs was significant for both Russia and America during the twentieth century.

Another important circumstance marked the profound difference between this and the earlier periods.

During the nineteenth century the common antagonism of the two nations toward Britain was often the cause of bringing them together. As far as the United States was concerned, the antagonistic feeling toward Britain was gradually becoming less of a factor in the determination of American foreign policy at the end of the nineteenth century. Since the '70's or '80's Britain had ceased to be a danger, and collaboration with her was becoming possible. The alliance of America with Britain in the two greatest wars in history marked the new century. During the twentieth century, therefore, Russian-American relations developed more independently of British policy.

On the whole, the relations of America and Russia in the new century were unsatisfactory. Of the forty-five years, ten or twelve at the most might be considered times of good relations (a few years beginning with 1905; 1915–17; 1934; and 1941–45); three quarters of Russian-American modern history was years of "unfriendly relations," which in 1918–19 manifested themselves in warlike operations, and in 1939–40 in warlike sentiments.

THE TWENTIETH CENTURY

THE present century began with violent attacks and mounting indignation against Russia on the part of the American Government as well as of American public opinion. The situation in the Far East was becoming a crucial factor in the relationship of the two nations, which suddenly found themselves rivals in the Pacific.

The one was advancing from the north, the other had become entrenched in the Philippines. Between them lay the great and at the same time weak body of China. The Chinese problem was becoming the main issue.

No greater controversy in the policies of the two powers could have arisen than the one over China. Britain, France, and Germany, also vitally interested in China, had each her own program and far-reaching ambitions; all were eager to acquire bases, concessions, railroads on Chinese territory. China's immediate neighbor, Russia, however, was far more expansionist than the others and its ambitions in the way of territorial acquisitions touched Chinese Turkestan, Mongolia, Manchuria, and Korea. The three European powers—Britain, France, and Germany—had to exercise some restraint and content themselves (because they had to operate mainly as naval powers) with ports, settlements, concessions, extraterritorial rights, and trade agreements. The United States was opposed to the imperialism of the Western powers in China and, to a still greater degree, to the Russian advance. Since Russia was becoming the strongest power in the Far East, it was natural that America, at the outset of her career as a great power, should side with the anti-Russian group, headed by Britain, and in which Japan was gradually becoming the most active member. Of course, no coalition or agreement bound the United States to Britain and Japan, but her policy was definitely in favor of the pronounced anti-Russian forces. Theodore Roosevelt's anti-Russian declarations were most daring and his tirades against the Tsar were remembered for a long time. When the Japanese attacked Russia in 1904, President Roosevelt was firmly resolved to enter the war on the side of Japan if any European power (Germany or France) gave military assistance to Russia. American public opinion was entirely on the side of Japan, since she appeared to be inferior to Russia in strength and in expansionist potentialities.[9]

American policy in the Far East was almost a pure balance of power policy. America's chief enemy was the strongest power of the Far East and she therefore sided with the adversaries of this power. After Russia's heavy defeats in the war from which Japan emerged the victor, Theodore Roosevelt became active in favor of a peace in order that Japan might not grow too strong. Peace was concluded at Portsmouth, New Hampshire, and resulted in a notable amelioration of Russo-American friction during the years following the war.

The good relations, however, lasted for only a few years. After 1908, when Russia resumed activity in the Far East, they gradually deteriorated. In 1911 the denunciation by the United States of the trade treaty which had been in operation between the two nations for eighty years marked the renewal of conflict. The official reason given for this move on the part of the United States Government was Russia's denial of

9. Russian-American relations in the Far East are discussed at length in Chapter VIII.

entry to American Jews, but the real causes lay, of course, in the new "climate" of mutual relations.

During the first World War Russia was a member of the allied powers from the very beginning. America's policy was favorable to the Allies and relations between Russia and the United States began to improve. American exports to Russia reached huge figures. Russian-American rapprochement reached its high point in 1917, when America entered the war and Russia overnight became a republic. Never before had relations been so good, particularly as far as public opinion was concerned. The rapport was marred, however, by the deterioration in Russia's military power because of the disintegration of her army, and by the inability of the young democracy to cope with both her external and internal enemies.

Then, at the beginning of the Soviet period, America intervened by force of arms in Russia. It was an undeclared war, but it was a war. The American forces were small compared with the French and British. They tried a "pro-democratic" course in Russia, but on the whole American intervention was halfhearted. Together with the British, the Americans occupied the Archangel region in 1918–19; with the Japanese, they intervened in the Far East at the same time.

Following the end of American armed intervention, there began a fourteen-year period of nonrecognition —1918–33—a period of semihostility and halfhearted unofficial relationship. Certainly neither armed intervention nor nonrecognition was a masterpiece of international policy. Even in the Far East, where the intervention was aimed primarily against the aspirations of Japan, it was an invasion of Russia's territory without her consent. And the nonrecognition of the Soviet Government by the United States, after the powers of Europe had resumed normal relations with the Soviet, was no act of political farsightedness. On the other hand, the opinion, so popular today, that at the bottom of all Russian-American difficulties down to the present lay the recollection of American intervention in Russia is not correct. After 1933 new events created new quarrels and tensions.

The idea of an American-Russian collaboration in the Far East (decisive for the new American policy toward Russia since 1933) did not materialize. The Soviet Government has never accepted the American concept of common action against Japan. Its view, on the contrary, advocated a balance of power between America and Japan, and conflicts between these two powers as a means of insuring Siberia's safety and of facilitating Soviet expansion in China. "When thieves fall out, the honest man wins," was Lenin's principle, in application to both Europe and Asia; his heirs remained true to this principle. When in 1937 Japan started her great invasion of China, the United States did not oppose her by force of arms, and Moscow was not at all inclined to enter into an anti-Japanese coalition.

American-Russian relations reached a new low in

1939, after the Moscow pact with Germany, and particularly after the start of the Soviet-Finnish War. The Soviet press was accusing America of hypocrisy. While professing to conduct a policy of neutrality in the European war, it was said in Moscow, the United States was actually rendering assistance to France and Britain. In Moscow's eyes America's offense lay in her pro-ally, anti-German attitude. "The policy of neutrality," the *Bolshevik*, wrote, in October, 1939, "is downright hypocrisy; especially so is the policy pursued by the greatest capitalist power—the USA . . . The bourgeois are outdoing themselves in trying to gain as much profit from the war as possible." The idea behind this accusation was: Britain is on the verge of defeat and disintegration, and the United States, her creditor, is striving to salvage her invested capital and to inherit as much as possible of the crumbling empire. The humorous magazine, *Crocodile*, published cartoons, one of which showed John Bull lying on his deathbed, and Uncle Sam sadly exclaiming, "He must not die, he owes me so much!" In another cartoon a ship representing Britain was shown sinking and John Bull trying to save his suitcases labeled "Canada" and "Australia"; Uncle Sam is addressing him from below, from a rescue boat: "Sir, throw down your trunks, you will feel lighter." "Appetite grows during neutrality," was the caption of a third cartoon.

These ideas were not inventions of individual writers. They were repeated everywhere and given elaborate economic interpretation through long articles in magazines and leading newspapers; it was obvious that these interpretations emanated from high places.

"Behind the veil of neutrality," the *Communist International* commented (1939, Nos. 8–9), "the American imperialists are fomenting war in the Far East . . . and promoting the European war, thus making the United States the military arsenal of England and France, and pocketing huge profits from bloodshed of the warring nations. She aims at crowding out her rivals from world markets, at consolidating her imperialistic positions, and at establishing domination on the seven seas."

Soviet antagonism toward American policy was due to American intervention in European affairs. What Moscow was demanding of the United States was a more perfect system of isolation. "The United States is feverishly preparing for war," the *Communist International* wrote in May, 1940. "The bourgeoisie of the United States is gambling on the attrition of the warring nations in order to be able at the last moment to dictate its will and to seize the lion's share of the spoils."

The annexation of the Baltic countries by the Soviet Union marked the height of political antagonism between Russia and the United States. The State Department declared on July 24, 1940, that the United States is "opposed to predatory activities" as well as to "any form of intervention on the part of one state, however powerful, in the domestic concerns of any other state, however weak." The American press almost unanimously supported the attitude of the government, while the Soviet press attacked the United States for hypocrisy. "American control of Cuba and the Philippines" served as proof that America was not too indisposed to "predatory activities." Foreign Commissar Molotov publicly replied to the State Department that although "there are certain people in the United States who are not pleased with the success of Soviet policy in the Baltic countries, we must confess we are little concerned over this fact inasmuch as we are coping with our tasks without the assistance of these disgruntled gentlemen."

Summer Welles, Under-Secretary of State, repeatedly warned the Soviet envoy in Washington that according to reliable information Germany was preparing to attack Russia in June, 1941.[10] In disclosing these facts to the Soviet Government the State Department obviously aimed at the establishment of closer ties with Russia against the Axis. Common antagonism to Germany and Japan could, Mr. Sumner Welles certainly supposed, lead to collaboration between Russia and the United States. The effect of his warnings was the converse of his aim: the Soviet Government concluded a neutrality pact with Japan, thus opening the road to her attack in the Pacific. The attempt to bring about a rapprochement between America and Russia had again failed.

On the whole, the period between the start of the

10. Davis and Lindley, *How War Came*, p. 175.

European war and Germany's attack on Russia belongs to the worst chapters in the history of Russian-American relations.

THE SECOND WORLD WAR

THE years following June, 1941, were ones of Russian-American alliance. If one were classifying the 160-years history of their relations according to good and bad periods, the four years from 1941 to 1945 would belong to the distinctly good. A common war, with common blood sacrifices, common triumphs and discouragements, and a common ruthless enemy, were bound to arouse popular sentiment as well as stimulate diplomatic activities of the best kind. Nothing is stronger in international relations than selfish interest. The selfish interests of the two nations, both at war with Germany, were motive enough for their close collaboration and mutual understanding. More than that, both were prepared to forget the conflicting issues of the past and even to condone what a short time before had been an evil and a crime.

American democracy was for the first time presented in Soviet Russia as a positive achievement, rather than a government of hypocrisy. Stalin praised America and England: "They possess elementary democratic liberties. There exist there trade-unions for workers and employees. There are workers' parties, and there is a Parliament." [11] The Atlantic Charter was signed by Russia, although not without reserva-

11. Speech, November 6, 1941.

tions. On many occasions "our gallant allies" were hailed by the Soviet press and in public declarations of Soviet leaders.

Similarly, in America, public opinion rapidly turned to approval of Soviet policies. Newspapers and their Moscow correspondents began to depict Soviet Russia in pleasant colors; dark spots were overlooked. The pro-Soviet trend of mind was winning adherents among nonpartisan Americans. The Soviet-German pact of 1939 was being presented as a logical sequence of the blunders of the democracies; the purges and trials in Russia were depicted as a cleaning of the Soviet house of German agents, in far-sighted preparation for the war. Criticism of Soviet policy was becoming taboo with numerous publications which otherwise had nothing to do with Communism. At the same time lend-lease supplies, in rapidly mounting quantities, were being shipped to Russia, with strong public approval.

Nevertheless, the war policies of a government are always a continuation of prewar policies. Between America and Russia questions were arising which marred the good relationship, and issues were emerging which contributed to discord. During the first two to three years of the war the main issue was the "second front." The fact that Russia's powerful allies were not invading Europe was attributed by the Soviet side to the fact that the capitalist governments of these nations, acting in the interest of their capitalist classes, were striving to prolong the war in order to prolong the industrial boom and swell war profits. There was no doubt in Russia that the invasion would eventually take place, since Stalin himself, in his report to the Moscow Soviet (November 6, 1942), retorted to those of his adherents who were in utter despair:

"In the opinion of these people the [Russian-Anglo-American] coalition consists of heterogeneous elements with different ideologies and this circumstance will prevent their organizing a joint action against the common enemy. I think this assertion is wrong. It would be ridiculous to deny the differences in ideologies and social systems of the countries composing the Anglo-Soviet-American coalition. But does this preclude the possibility and expediency of joint action? It certainly does not."

However, according to the Soviet view, the interests of American capitalists were straining against a too speedy conclusion of the war. In numerous articles and speeches this idea was cautiously presented to the public and the interpretation given it was that in the interim millions of Soviet citizens would have to die in order to enable American industrialists to amass fortunes.

In *War and the Working Class* (January 15, 1944) M. J. Okov described his trip through America which took him from San Francisco to New York. His long narrative, otherwise of little interest, was obviously written to publish the following conversation (composed, of course, by the author or the editor) which he allegedly had with a certain capitalist:

"I was puzzled by a statement of a big industrialist, owner of a big tool plant. At a banquet he addressed the following question to me: 'Why are you Russians trying to end the war as soon as possible?'

"I was stunned by this question and thought he was joking. Thousands of human beings were perishing, hundreds of towns and villages were being destroyed, untold treasures of cultural value were being demolished. It seemed strange to have to mention this.

"Noticing my amazement, the industrialist waved his hand and said: 'I am aware of all this. What of it? Never mind. Towns and villages can be rebuilt, cultural values can be brought or new ones ordered which will be better than the old ones. As for people—there are plenty of them everywhere. Take China: Look at the number of men and women who are idle. It wouldn't do any harm if the population decreased somewhat. There will be more births to make up for it. Don't you realize? I have not seen times like these in thirty years. What a demand, what business! Do you imagine that under such circumstances I favor a speedy end of the war? No! Why am I here, in this gathering of the United Nations? Because I support the United Nations. In this war Hitler and his friend Musso must perish. This is clear. You want it, and all the United Nations want it. But why rush? That isn't necessary!' "

A few weeks later the same official magazine published an article by Professor M. Bogolepov describing the "stock exchange boom" in the United States during the war. It stressed the fact that prices on the exchange rose when a long war was anticipated, and dropped when an early end of the war seemed probable. The inherent political idea was expressed thus:

"Can it be assumed that all the representatives of moneyed interests, all the noblemen of finance and the kings of industry wish the complete destruction of fascism? This is doubtful, to say the least." The editors of the magazine added a note to Bogolepov's article concerning the "political influence exercised by moneyed circles."

The notion that capitalist classes (in America and England) were akin, in a way, to fascism and would endeavor to save the remnants of fascism after the war was prevalent in Soviet circles. The institutions created by America and Britain for the control of the Axis countries (the so-called AMG) or for the rehabilitation of liberated lands (UNRRA) were suspected of capitalist fascist tendencies. "The administration [of liberated countries] is being organized upon principles which have nothing in common with democracy." "American food supplies are already being used as a political weapon. The weapon is being used for the support of some circles in the Vichy Government. It is being used for the support of monarchists and certain fascist groups in the Franco government, and of his regime." [12]

Other political differences, too, disturbed the al-

12. *War and the Working Class*, September, 1943, and January, 1944.

liance during the first three war years, such as the barring of foreign correspondents from the front lines in Russia, rigid censorship, failure of the Soviet press to acknowledge the full extent of allied assistance to Russia, and particularly the nonapplication of the Atlantic Charter to the Baltic States and eastern Poland.

Early in 1944 discussion concerning the "second front" gradually subsided, as a decision had been taken concerning it by the leaders of the powers at the Teheran Conference. Meanwhile, with the German Armies suffering defeats and in the process of withdrawing from Russia, other problems were rising to the surface—problems more fundamental than the issues which had been dividing the allies during the first years of war. Poland's future was the chief question, but of great importance also were the divergent attitudes on the punishment of war criminals, division of Germany into zones of occupation, the future of the Balkans, the creation of "spheres of interest" in Europe. The exigencies of the war compelled the allied governments to seek compromises, which were subsequently reached, the United States Government making important concessions to Soviet points of view. Public opinion in America, however, while in general approving the necessity of concessions, was beginning to be uneasy concerning the course of Russian policy.

Dissatisfaction was occasionally expressed in the Soviet press also. The official publications, while avoiding any direct criticism of President Roosevelt or of the government of the United States, attacked American political leaders for their views, which more often than not were the views of the White House. Wendell Willkie, for instance, was attacked for his stand on the Polish problem; the *New York Times,* for its opposition to Soviet expansionism; and the *Times* military observer, Hanson Baldwin, for his alleged tendency to see the European war as ending in attrition. Repeated press attacks were aimed at the former American Ambassador to Russia, William C. Bullitt, at the Scripps-Howard newspapers, and, of course, at the Hearst, Patterson, and McCormick publications.

During the last stages of the war Russian-American relations were still good as far as military affairs were concerned; they were erratic and unsatisfactory in purely political matters: the Russian attitude toward Americans in the "Soviet sphere"; the Soviet policy in Poland; the deep antagonism between Moscow and the Vatican—these and many other questions were a source of growing disagreement, although the Administration was prepared to make great concessions to Moscow.

No sooner had Germany capitulated than American-Russian relations again began quickly to deteriorate. The shift was sharp and rapid, as if history desired to demonstrate that the alliance of the Big Three had been a purely wartime combination.

During the first month following the end of the war with Germany the Soviet Armies completed occupation of the east and north of Germany and made a closed frontier of the line of demarcation between the

Soviet sphere in Germany and the zones of the Western allies. The Danish island of Bornholm, guarding the entrance to the Baltic, was likewise occupied. No demobilization of the army was decreed in Moscow, and the new pro-Soviet Polish Army continued to organize. General Boček, the leader of the new Czech Army, announced that it would undergo training in Russia and would be equipped by the Soviets. "Our army," he said, on May 19, eleven days after the armistice, "will grow in battle. . . . The army is destined for battle; battle is its aim." Tito's Yugoslav Army occupied Italian Trieste and a province in southern Austria; following American and British protests, only the latter occupation was abandoned. The general uneasiness was growing.

At the San Francisco Conference of the United Nations, which was in session at the time, relations between the Soviet delegation and the Americans and British were strained. They sank to a low point when Molotov disclosed that the sixteen Polish leaders who, on American and British advice, had presented themselves to Soviet authorities for purposes of negotiating, had been arrested and indicted. Sensing a challenge in this action, the London and Washington governments asked Moscow for an explanation, but Moscow refused to discuss the question, making a brusque reply to London, a politer one to Washington. No more successful were the negotiations concerning a government for Austria which followed the setting up, without consultation with the allies, of the

Soviet-sponsored Renner government in Vienna.

At the end of May Harry Hopkins again went to Moscow to seek a solution to the vexing problems. Everything appeared to move in the direction of Anglo-American rapprochement and a widening of the gap separating America and Britain from the Soviet leadership—unless a new combination, growing out of interest in the Far East, should temporarily revive the wartime coalition.

A SUMMARY

For one hundred and sixty years American-Russian relations have developed along an irregular course, at times achieving genuine collaboration, at other times sinking to outright military conflict.

So long as the activity of the two nations was limited to local or regional interests, neither serious conflict nor close collaboration could arise, unless a common opposition to a third power would temporarily bring them together.

When one of the two nations advanced to the status of a world power—it was Russia in the first half of the nineteenth century—the chances of conflict became stronger because of potential and occasionally actual encroachment and intervention on the part of the stronger power in territories and spheres of the other nation. Subsequent (after 1856) limitation of the Russian political sphere to Eastern Europe and Asia re-created the basis for good relations.

When both nations began to move as great powers

in world politics (after 1898) the chances of conflict arising between them grew, since the Far East was now included as a disputed sphere of interests. However, the period during which both America and Russia were simultaneously acting as great powers has been less than thirty years in the course of a century and a half (1898–1917 and 1935–45), and in some of these years the growth of Germany has overshadowed all other issues.

After the first World War Russia ceased to play the role of a great power. When she returned to the status of a great power at the end of the '30's, it was again Germany that commanded her chief attention and, somewhat later, that of the United States. And, again, common antagonism to Germany brought the nations together in a military alliance.

There is nothing, therefore, in the history of American-Russian relations which in itself can be reassuring for the future. There can be no automatic adjustment and readjustment of their interests. There is no cureall for possible conflict. Everything depends on the political course voluntarily chosen by the two nations: in the old world—in the heart of Europe; in the new sphere of conflicts—in China, Korea, and Japan; and in the third sore spot of world politics—in the Middle East.

X

CONCLUSION

ND then, when the shooting is over in all parts of the globe, and the smoke of battle has lifted, a tormented world will lie at the feet of the victors, a score of helpless, miserable nations, covered with wounds. None of them except the Big Three will have any real power in international affairs, and there will be no power of resistance against the Big Ones. There will seem to be no limit to the force of their arms. The situation will be unique.

Following a great war new and often unexpected trends and tendencies appear among the peoples of the victorious nations. Trends toward expansion, toward creation of new great empires, toward extension of spheres to include weaker nations, are bound to arise in every one of the victorious peoples. Whether or not such tendencies will become strong will depend on many circumstances; but jingoism and militarism will be present and will attract public attention.

The germs of such trends already exist, and it would be easy even today to point to the public leaders and the writers who are destined to be the spokesmen for them. The necessary ideas will be supplied; the needed slogans will be created. No political trend has ever remained silent for lack of slogans or ideology.[1]

The British trend, after every war, has been toward the acquisition of new colonies, peoples, and spheres. No new ideas would be needed to prolong the old line into the future; an axiom does not require an explanation. However, the complete change in Britain's international position may, by virtue of necessity rather than modesty, preclude any large-scale British imperialist expansion.

Will the United States inherit this trend, together with some other of John Bull's traits? Or will she be able to resist the temptation?

The Dutch East Indies, potentially so rich, are an empire in themselves. Their tin, oil, and rubber will be of great importance in the postwar period. Their geographical location is strategic. Near-by Thailand, up to now an important center of Japanese activity, will fall to the Anglo-Saxon powers. The French

1. An example may be cited. A National Legion of the American People, recently created in the state of Pennsylvania, is claiming (a) all possessions held by European nations in the Western hemisphere, except Canada; (b) the Dutch Indies, the Malayan Peninsula, and all possessions held by the European powers in the Pacific; and, of course, (c) the Pacific islands held by Japan. The League is neither large nor important, but the trend of its thinking is characteristic: the American people must wake up to demand "a part of their [the allies] empires in repayment for what we have done for them . . . American lives and American wealth saved Great Britain, liberated France and are now liberating the Netherlands. What are we getting for it? Love and kisses? These may delight and satisfy the President, the State Department, and their followers in and out of Congress. But not the rest of us!" *Bulletin* No. 1.

Government has exerted some military effort to re-conquer Indo-China; but essentially Indo-China will be rewon by American and British forces. This corner of the world, between Australia and China and on the road from the Indian to the Pacific Ocean, is a spot where the colonial and other interests of Britain, France, America, and Holland meet. Together these countries of Southern Asia embrace a population of over 110 millions. In Africa the Italian colonies lie in the vicinity of the traditional British sphere; other lands belong to Portugal and Belgium.

Schemes for internationalization of possessions of the defeated powers as well as of certain lands of the allies may loom important. For the United States, a newcomer in many areas, the best way of preventing unilateral dominance of lands and peoples by old co-lonial powers would be to put them under a collective organization in which the United States would actu-ally assume the leading role. To such a scheme there would be strong resistance on the part of the old mas-ters, with Britain at their head; however, there is the possibility that the United States would receive sup-port from another aspirant—Soviet Russia. A redivi-sion of colonies and continents may produce new and unexpected, though not lasting, groupings of powers.

Following great victories people are often inclined to minimize the complications and dangers involved in large-scale imperialism, and to exaggerate the import-ance of guns and mortars for use in peacetime. They often do not realize that coercion, punitive expeditions, opposition to popular movements and uprisings, and new, unnecessary wars are the sequel of depriving other peoples of their independence. Whether this extension of imperialism will arise in America and Britain, and, if so, how strong it will become after the war, is a question for the future. So far this point of view has not assumed any important place in the political opinions of the peoples of these two nations.

In Russia the new trend has already been successful. A great uneasiness concerning Russia's postwar aims has been felt in all parts of the world, including the countries of Russia's allies, and this uneasiness has been mounting from month to month since 1943. It is based on facts. After Stalingrad uncertainty as to the outcome of the war was beginning to fade in Russia, and new plans for postwar settlements matured rapidly. Beginning modestly, proposals of territorial settlements grew more and more ambitious. Limited at the beginning to a few neighboring territories, they gradually began to include great lands and peoples. Slogans and ideas sprang up spontaneously: crushing of fascism; guarantee of Russian security; prevention of future wars; transformation of social systems.

Absence of criticism from within the nation facilitated the growth of these political sprouts, which were rooted deeply in the prevailing ideology. The conviction that dangers which have confronted other powers in their programs of expansion do not exist in the case of the Soviet Union; the intoxication over military victories; the minimizing of the allies' assistance in the war and of the quantity of supplies which they furnished to Russia; the conviction that the German defeat was accomplished almost exclusively by Russia; the feeble resistance on the part of the allies to Soviet policy in Central Europe; the support on the part of numerous elements within the allied nations; the unprecedented plenary authority of the supreme Soviet leader—all these were pushing Russia on the road of widening the Soviet state, its spheres of influence, and its "security zones" in all three of the sore spots of international relations. Hence arose the specter of the "third war" which has been haunting the world now for two years.

The menace has not abated in the meantime. The same blindness that befell America on the eve of the first World War, when Andrew Carnegie, after his visit to Berlin, assured the world of the strictly pacifist intentions of the Kaiser, and the same blindness that was prevalent ten years ago, when the American public was not inclined to believe that Germany was taking a deliberate course leading to conflict, has been manifest during the last several years.

Stalin would indeed not be deserving of the title of a great leader of his movement were he to relinquish his yearning to do away everywhere with inimical social and political groups and simultaneously to extend the Soviet social structure to near-by peoples and states; were he not to do everything in his power to replace the vague constitution of the vague United

Conclusion

Nations organization with the cement of that other entity of United Nations—the USSR; were he not to apply any and all means to achieve these goals. No sermons or persuasion can halt this aim; no compliments paid to Stalin's wisdom can change the course of events; no silence about the impending dangers can remove them. Stalin's numerous political concessions made and then retracted during the last two decades evidence his skill as a master of politics. The policy of the Soviet Government during the years 1923 to 1939, when the force in the hands of the other powers was overwhelming, was a policy of peace. Great force is the most eloquent argument for peace; it speaks louder than charters and covenants. The coming period in world history will be, at best, a period of armed peace.

But when things have gone too far, even the will to forestall the developing conflicts may prove futile. Europe is a peculiar conglomerate of nations governed by certain immutable laws. If you are a great power in Europe, you can win wars and territories and expand your rule, but only up to a certain limit; if you have exceeded this limit, if you have swallowed too much, you cannot stop, you must go further. The resentment of the menaced nations, military preparations on the part of the big powers, world-wide uneasiness, drive you to ever new campaigns, even if you clearly see the danger in them. In Europe you may possess your part of the continent, perhaps a little more than your part. You cannot, however, possess half of Europe; if you do, the unwritten law of Europe prescribes that you must take all the rest. What is at stake then is all or nothing.

To the political genius of Napoleon the dangers of a war with Russia were obvious. He spoke about the coming war on Russia as if it were destiny. By his own victories he had pushed reluctant Russia to Britain's side; Russia's war against Napoleon became Europe's war of liberation and was disastrous for Napoleon. The dilemma which he faced was all of Europe or nothing. The answer was—nothing. Hitler, although smaller in stature than Napoleon, also certainly saw the dangers involved in his Russian campaign before he started it, but, with the other half of Europe at his feet, the race could not be stopped. It was not blindness that drove him to Kiev and Stalingrad; it was rather a logical and inevitable necessity.

Today it is still possible for the Soviet Union to retreat in Europe to the limits of national Russia—to the natural borders of the three main Russian nationalities —and to reëstablish the real independence of her neighbors. Tomorrow may be too late. No amount of realism and sober calculation is of any help when a certain limit of power expansion has been crossed, when a concession starts to look like a defeat, when the rest of the world has become nervously militant. Ultimate defeat of the expanding power becomes certain.

For more than three decades Russia has been tossing painfully between the two extremes of unprecedented expansion into Europe and unprecedented retreat into the heart of the eastern plains. During the early stages of the first World War the Russian Empire, with Finland and the greater part of Poland as components of it, unlocked Prussia and Austria and pushed forward to extend its area far into the middle of Europe. About three years later a peace was concluded which deprived Russia of her western and southern areas— Poland and Finland, as well as the Ukraine and Byelorussia, were lost. War was going on in the east, too, and the area under control of Moscow shrank until it comprised only a few central provinces. A great part of the lost territory was subsequently recovered. Then, in 1939–40, another great push into the west again considerably widened the sphere of the Russian state, from the Baltic to the Black Sea; 23 million people were incorporated. The next year, 1941–42, a reverse movement took place. The east and south were occupied by the enemy. Seventy million people fell under his rule. In this respect the events of the years 1941–42 bore a striking resemblance to those of 1918. The depths were reached again.

And then, since 1943, once more the torrents of Russian might streamed far into the west. No resistance to it was possible. The counterpressure, however, is bound to appear.

How long will this last? Is it an inevitable process that these unending expansion-and-contraction movements succeed one another? Every yard on the thousands of miles of road back and forth was bought by

human blood, by misery beyond imagination, by starvation of women and children. Is there an end in sight
for the tormented nation?

The end certainly depends not on Russia alone. But
so far as Russian policy is concerned, the excruciating
tossing about cannot end before healthy and normal
conditions prevail in the European East: that is, first,
the European sphere under Russian control ceases to
embrace peoples historically and ethnographically
alien; and, second, when the Russian sphere embraces
the whole of the three Russian nationalities—Great
Russians, Ukrainians, and Byelorussians.[2] Every attempt to deprive Russia of any part of her national
territories bears the seeds of new conflicts. Every attempt on Russia's part to widen to any considerable
extent her rule in Europe inevitably and naturally pro-
vokes a bellicose reaction. Only ethnographical frontiers can be stable frontiers, at least in the case of
Europe. They can be established voluntarily. If they
are not, they will be established by force.

Nations other than the Big Three will soon arise,
acquire influence and importance and make their impress, too, on the development of the postwar world.
Young nations are maturing, growing muscles, and
developing adult voices. Their potential spheres are
enormous. Australia, shooting up with American

2. The vexing question of eastern Poland is, actually, a question of Russia's internal political system. There cannot be any
doubt that were the political conditions different, a free ballot
in that region would be overwhelmingly in favor of Russia.

speed, will soon be interested in Oceania, in the West Indies, and in Southeastern Asia, where Dutch, French, British, and American interests meet. Since she will not soon become a great power, Australia will have to play her great role locally in that large region; she will make use of all the advantages of her ties with Britain and America, and of her position as the only white nation in the great area from India to Japan. She will have to function as the main agent of the Anglo-Saxon powers in her sphere, and will grow fast with this new assignment. No decision against Australia in this large region will be lasting. Her importance for the near future, so far as her part of the world is concerned, cannot be exaggerated.

South Africa is growing at a rapid rate on the colonial continent, in the vicinity of Portuguese, Belgian, French, and British possessions. Whether or not there is a redivision of colonies in the near future, her influence will radiate far into the north. Today she is already the strongest and richest nation of Africa, and her importance is bound to increase.

In Europe, France will rise again to the stature of a great power, although she will probably never be as great as she was in past centuries. It will take years to resurrect her military force. With or without assistance from abroad, she will have her large army under the traditionally excellent military leadership. This task will be facilitated for her by the paradoxical circumstance that her human losses in this war were minimal in comparison with those of any other power in Europe. France has long been out of the race for sea power. She will not reëstablish in full her former importance in the non-European world. As far as Europe is concerned, however, France emerges as the first power, after Russia, with her distinct and specific interests reaching far into the center and into the east of the Old World. Within a few years, France's voice in continental affairs is bound to become at least as important as Britain's.

The defeat suffered by Germany leaves that nation crushed, partitioned, and powerless. Her military strength is gone. She has nothing to say in European affairs, not to speak of world affairs. This is not her first defeat, however. After every earlier defeat she was able to rise again, as other nations have risen after crushing blows. Germany's main strength will lie in her economy, in her geographical situation, in the capabilities of her people. Europe needs German industry; without the economy of her most industrialized nation of the prewar period, Europe will be poorer. Restoration of Germany's railroads will be an urgent necessity for her neighbors; her coal will be required all over the west and south; her machines will be needed for the restoration of the economy all over the continent; her products are cheaper than American products; she knows the markets in detail. Germany will have much to restore in foreign lands, but a cow cannot be used for milk and slaughter at the same time. Therefore some of the economic restrictions imposed on Germany at first will have to be relaxed soon.

Conclusion

A degree of influence in European politics will be reacquired by Germany, after a certain time, by economic means. After 1918 the military force of Germany was negligible and remained so until 1933. However, after the middle '20's Germany did play a role in international relations, and it was her rapidly restored economy that was the basis of her rise. Difficult as will be the resurrection of German industry after 1945, the process will be essentially the same, though at first special efforts will be taken to prevent it. New leaders will arise, new political ideas will take shape in Germany; but Germany—a Germany of quite another type—has not been struck out as a political factor in the future.

Moreover, rivalry among the powers may provide opportunity for Germany to reacquire a dangerous amount of force. Throughout history, a similar situation has often made it possible for defeated nations to rise again. France, defeated and occupied by the armies of the allies in 1815, three years later was restored to her place among the leading powers. Even Hitler's rise would have been impossible had it not been for the antagonism between Germany's west and east, and between Britain and France. Harsh treatment of the vanquished, emotionally an intelligible requirement, in the case of Germany is no guarantee against a possible future German threat. Everything will depend on collaboration and antagonisms among the powers. Flaws in the relations between the big powers are the roads to strength and might for the weak ones.

The same pattern applies to Japan. Even if defeated and ousted from the Asiatic continent, Japan will remain a great economic organism. Her abilities in the economic field are surprising; her achievements all over the East are spectacular. In Asia and Oceania her trade has equaled that of the United States. Manchuria has developed, under Japan, at an amazing rate. This source of influence on international affairs will remain with Japan. In addition, her geographical location, at the very knot of Far Eastern troubles, can soon make her either an important buffer state among the big powers or even an ally—with all the privileges of a favorite of a big power. An end will be set, of course, to her dream of predominance over the continent of Asia and the Pacific, but Japanese influence in her own part of the world will not be eliminated altogether.

The predominance of the Big Three cannot be durable. A wartime combination, it will end soon after the war. A number of other nations will gradually climb the stairs to the big-power throne, and then new groupings, combinations, and coalitions will emerge.

If this is to be so, was it all futile—the sacrifices, the corpses, the cities reduced to rubble, nations in mourning, thousands of ships at the bottom of the seas? It was not. The war, a purely destructive job, had the great but limited aim of crushing genuine world conquerors, oppressors of alien peoples, slave drivers of the twentieth century. It was a great fight, although one with a purely negative aim. How great it was, those nations can tell which have been subjected to the rule of the conquerors. A greater accomplishment than this cannot be expected from a war. The war did not eradicate the divergences of international interests, it did not abolish coalitions and alliances, rivalry and power politics. It did not achieve these goals because no war can achieve them.

And so the world today is pretty far from having accomplished these lofty aims. Real progress can be achieved only in peace through internal evolution within each nation, after the external obstacles have been eliminated by the victory. In our times no absolute remedy exists against the menace of war, but the bloody history of two great world conflicts has proved that absolutism and tyranny constitute the best breeding ground of martial adventurers and geniuses of predatory war. Freedom is no absolute remedy against warlike tendencies, but lack of freedom promotes the growth of the martial spirit. Dictatorship is the high road to war. Conversely, the existence of political freedom and civil liberties acts as a brake on tendencies toward conquest and subjugation of alien nations.

Hitlerism is crushed, Fascism is dead. Their Japanese counterpart will follow them soon. Now a threat of war emanates from those absolutist political systems which still remain, which put their aims above right, their concepts above treaties, their might above international agreements, and make a scrap of paper of world-wide organizations. Genuine progress can be achieved only if in the immediate postwar years there is an internal rebuilding of these nations by forces within them. A peaceful period of constructive work and progress will not begin for the tormented humanity that has survived our world wars until that reconstruction has taken place.

Real progress can be achieved only through abolition, down to the last vestige, of internal political suppression and subjection, of all forms of autocracy, in the soil of which warlike tendencies and lust to conquest are bound to ripen. Progress will be possible only in a world really free, and only if the Wars of Liberation are succeeded by a real Peace of Liberation.

INDEX

Index

Index

Index